LONDON'S
LOST BATTLEFIELDS

LONDON'S
LOST BATTLEFIELDS
BOUDICCA TO WORLD WAR I

ROBERT BARD

FONTHILL

To my granddaughter Chloe Keen, and James and Harry Philipp

Previous page: Old London Bridge drawbridge gate, 1428, from *c.* 1550 drawing.

FONTHILL MEDIA
www.fonthillmedia.com

First published 2013

A CIP catalogue record for this book is available from the British Library

Typeset in 10.5pt on 12pt Adobe Caslon Pro
Typesetting by Fonthill Media
Printed in the UK

ISBN 978-1-78155-248-3

Contents

Acknowledgements

This book owes much to the assistance offered by the Battlefield Trust, and in particular the following members who went out of their way to assist, answer queries, and in a sense take me under their wing. In particular, I would like to thank Frank Baldwin, Harvey Watson, Julian Humphreys, Peter Burley, and Mike Elliot. For his assistance with the Boudicca section, Martin Marix Evans. With regards locating the head of Simon of Sudbury, who perished in the Peasants' Revolt, I would like to thank the Revd Canon Gregory Webb of St Gregory's Church, Sudbury, for good humoured patience and for letting me photograph the head. The chapter on the Battle of St Albans owes much to Peter Burley and Mike Elliot. I would also like to thank Tom Entwistle, a descendent of Sir Bertine Entwistle, a knight who fought at that battle, for his assistance. With regards the Battle of Barnet, again the members of the Battlefield Trust were extremely helpful, as was Brian Warren, who gave me much time and was patient in answering my queries on the locations of landmarks and positions of the warring factions. I'd like to thank Ian Southern for his encouragement, and finally, Les Abrahams, who found the locations and in particular researched the chapter on the First World War, and who as ever acted with good humour and patience when I had lost mine.

Introduction

London over the centuries has been the focus of a number of significant battles and uprisings. Many parts of London, her suburbs, and surrounding towns bear silent witness to some of the worst savageries that one person can inflict on another. Most of the many tens of thousands who participated, certainly in the earlier uprisings, lie in unknown graves, perhaps waiting through development and archaeological research to be rediscovered.

What I have looked to do in *Battlefield London* is give the reader an insight into causes of the more important uprisings and battles that took place in London and some of the roads into London. Where available, I have used sources that date from the time of the battle or uprising, and where available, participant accounts. There is something emotionally and historically satisfying about standing in the exact spot that an early eyewitness stood on and witnessed or participated in an event that happened centuries earlier. Often buildings, churches, open land, and streets remain in a recognisable form and act as a sounding board from the distant past.

As a rule, the earlier the battle, the less we know. When Boudicca (the name means 'Victory'; I prefer Boadicea) revolted against the Romans in AD 61, she left little that was tangible nearly 2,000 years later except a layer of burnt substance in the appropriate archaeological stratum of Colchester, Verulamium (St Albans), and London. The Roman author Cornelius Tacitus,[1] born *c.* AD 56, is our only useful source for the Boudiccan revolt. There is a later reference to the rebellion by Cassius Dio (*c.* AD 164-235), but his main source was probably Tacitus. Both Tacitus and Dio's works were lost to history, as was Boudicca, until she was rediscovered during the Renaissance by the historian Polydore Virgil in 1534. Boudicca, as 'Boadicea', underwent resurgence during the Victorian period

The Victorian heroine: Boadicea and her daughters, Westminster Bridge. The statue was commissioned by Prince Albert and executed by Thomas Thornycroft.

as the subject of a poem by Tennyson. The bronze statue with her daughters at Westminster Bridge shows her as a conquering heroine. She has become a national heroine despite how very little is known about her.

With regards to the final battle between Boudicca and the Roman Governor Suetonius, its location is the subject of a large amount of speculative literature that has developed on the basis of a minimal number of lines from Tacitus: 'He [Suetonius] chose a position in a defile with a wood behind him. There could be no enemy, he knew, except at his front, where there was open countryside without cover for ambushes.'[2] Following this simple observation, which could apply to numerous parts of England, layers of folklore and supposition as to where the final battle was fought, covering London and surrounding counties, has been established. It is conceivable that one day a chance discovery will reveal the true location. One of the exciting elements of early battlefield archaeology is the unveiling of history when a surprise find leads to certainty of location. One such example was the discovery of an early battle, recounted by both Tacitus and Dio, in Germany, where Rome suffered its worst defeat ever: three Legions, comprising between 15,000 and 20,000 soldiers, were massacred. The defeat was believed to have taken place in the Teutowald Forest, north of Osnabruck, in September AD 9. There was, however, little or no proof of location until a British amateur archaeologist found a couple of Roman catapult projectiles and coins in 1987.

Archaeologists have since excavated a part of the battlefield at a place called Kalkriese in the Teutowald. Discoveries have included Roman swords and

Above and below: Finds from the Battle of the Teutoburg Forest. Above is a ceremonial mask found at Kalkriese. Below is the group of slingshots found by the British amateur archaeologist Major Tony Clunn in summer 1988, which led to the discovery of the battlefield site.

daggers, parts of javelins and spears, arrowheads, sling stones, fragments of helmets, a mask, nails of soldiers' sandals, belts, bits of chain mail, and fragments of armour. In 1994, the first human remains were discovered, and in the following years several mass graves were uncovered.[3] A comprehensive visitor centre has now opened – proof that a battle that took place nearly half a century before the defeat of Boudicca in similar climatic conditions could still be discovered, identified, and excavated in this country.[4]

Even some of the later battlegrounds, such as that of the Battle of Barnet[5] from 1471 (see Chapter Five), have yet to be located. We have accounts from within days of the battle that put it somewhere on the Great North Road, between 0.5 and 1 mile north of Barnet, with a few enigmatic clues thrown in. Somewhere, around 1 mile or so north of the town of Barnet, under a field next to a now-lost chantry chapel, lie the bodies of between 3,000 and 4,000 forgotten soldiers of the Wars of the Roses. We know with a reasonable level of probability where the chantry chapel was located. At some stage, the Battlefield Trust, an organisation dedicated to the preservation of Britain's battlefields, will begin the process that will hopefully lead to the locating of the battlefield site and the placing of boards to show visitors where the battle took place.

In recent years, the site of the Battle of Bosworth in Leicestershire was relocated by using field walkers and detectorist groups in conjunction with specialist battlefield archaeologists under one of Britain's leading battlefield archaeologists, Glenn Foard. They were able to identify musket shot, arrowheads, and cannon balls as being of the right type, found in quantity in the right places.[6] This, in conjunction with a reinterpretation of original accounts, has in the past been a recipe for success; Locating the sites of urban battlefields is often far more precise. Early accounts will often speak of crossing a river and battling through a barricade in a certain part of a town, where fighting took place in a market place, and so on. This is what happened during the Wars of the Roses in St Albans. Old maps and eyewitness accounts then allowed us to say with a large degree of certainty that King Henry VI raised his banner for battle to commence in the immediate vicinity of what is now the Boots store in the market place in St Albans, that the Earl of Warwick (the Kingmaker) in the same battle attacked with a force of men through the bar area of The Keys public house, and that the Duke of Somerset was slain opposite the Skipton building society. This, in conjunction with the fact that so many original buildings still stand (reference made to these buildings is what makes a well laid out battlefield walk so interesting) means we can connect with dramatic events from the past, stand where they took place, and try to picture what it must have been like to observe or take part in those events. I have deliberately included St Albans, which lies just over 20-miles north of central London on Watling Street (A5) where two well documented battles took place: the opening battle of the Wars of the Roses in 1455 and a second, much more destructive battle in the same dynastic struggle in 1461.

It seems appropriate in writing a book that deals primarily with battlefields of earlier times that a chapter be devoted to looking briefly at myth versus reality. Battlefields were not noble, swashbuckling places where conflicting parties fought bravely and to a code of honour. They were places of extreme violence, where fear, terror, and self-preservation predominated. It is no coincidence that the majority of those that perished as a result of battle died while in flight, not in face to face combat. It was common for fleeing combatants to discard armour and weapons to make flight easier. This made them vulnerable to the inevitable chasing cavalry that saw post-battle killing as part of the sport of warfare. Not only do we have contemporary accounts and pictures of what took place on the battlefield and after the battle, but in recent years a number of combatant skeletons have been unearthed, many of which show horrific injuries, including death and dismemberment in its most unimaginable and nightmarish form. Set piece battles tended to be short in duration, rarely lasting more than 4 hours, as exhaustion set in. Certainly up until and beyond the English Civil War, as the commander of a unit of soldiers one could never be certain that the foot soldiers behind you would not flee the field at the first sign of trouble, or would even be there when you looked round. It was not uncommon for parts of an army to change sides mid-battle; treachery was always in the air. Up until the first phase of the Wars of the Roses, it was common to spare ones enemy after a victory, or to 'give quarter', a term used to accept surrender. Looting of nearby towns or wagon trains would invariably be the reward or incentive for the victorious side, and important prisoners would be held hostage for suitably rewarding ransoms; fortunes could be made by all ranks. This changed during the Wars of the Roses. Its very intense dynastic nature, whereby noble family lost close relatives, led to a strong desire for revenge. It became customary for the key participants of the losing side to be summarily despatched after the battle. Orders were sometimes given that the ordinary foot soldiers should not be spared either. Parts of London suffered terribly at the hands of pre-Second World War victors. The revolts of 1381 and 1450 were both destructive, leaving palls of smoke over London and the suburbs. Brentford suffered at the hands of Prince Rupert after being sacked, or so Parliamentarian propaganda had it.

Particularly satisfying in terms of researching and following the routes of uprising and struggle were the 1381 Peasants Revolt and the 1450 Jack Cade rebellion. Both are commemorated by street names on Blackheath. The sites of death and destruction take in many of London's key landmarks, and some relatively unexplored corners. Both rebellions caused major changes in the very nature of English feudal society and led to new boundaries being set between the government and the governed. To walk the routes of the two rebellions is to take in some of London's most famous landmarks, past and present.

London was the site of two English Civil Wars battles. One already mentioned, which took place at Brentford and the next day nearby at Turnham

Green. These took place on 12 and 13 November 1642 respectively. Again, thanks to the Battlefield Trust, both sites have been comprehensively researched and sign-boarded to allow an interesting and informed tour of the sites, which include nearby Syon House, the London home of the Duke of Northumberland. The house was attacked during the Royalist attack on Brentford. As we come so close into London it is a pleasant surprise to note that so much that is original in terms of landscapes and buildings that survive, including the mustering point for Charles I's army on Hounslow Heath, which despite low flying aircraft, remains atmospheric, unspoiled, and in a form that would almost certainly still be recognisable to the seventeenth century combatants.

It is well to remember when enjoying some of the pre-First World War battlefields referred to in this book that battlefield sites, because of their ethereal nature and coverage of often valuable land, suffer from lack of legal protection and are often subject to development proposals. It was the likelihood of a road being gouged through the site of the 1645 English Civil War Battle of Naseby in Leicestershire that inspired the creation of the Battlefields Trust in 1993. The trust states:

> The spur to set up the trust was the fact that the battlefield of Naseby, then a perfectly preserved site of the decisive battle of the English Civil War, was to be bisected with a motorway link during 1992, the 350th anniversary year of the English Civil War. In any listing of the top twenty most important battlefields of the world, Naseby would appear. Never again would people be able to appreciate this battlefield in its entirety and follow the line of Prince Rupert's charge and his attack on the Parliamentary baggage train, an action [that] deprived King Charles of the bulk of his cavalry at the crucial moment of the battle – as his infantry were being surrounded.[7]

In recent years there has been an increasing interest amongst historians, archaeologists, and a number of universities in all aspects of battlefields that has led to the discipline of battlefield archaeology emerging as a separate field of archaeology in its own right. It comes with many subdivisions, all focused on bringing alive not only the history of the battles themselves, but through the examination of skeletons and artefacts found, life and living at the times of the battles. In 2005, an extensive document, entitled 'Battlefield Archaeology : a guide to the archaeology of conflict,'[8] was issued, which acknowledged that the time had come to lay down certain guidelines. There are a number of interesting comments in the document:

> It is [...] of the greatest importance to accurately record the locations of where the combatants from a conflict lie. The strength of feeling regarding war cemeteries and the popularity of historic battlefields, particularly invoked by the media and the current trend to destroy sites of conflict, suggest that the general public support the study of battlefields through their educational,

financial and emotional involvement [...] 'battlefield touring is now one of the world's fastest growing leisure activities'. However, if a battlefield is not a pleasant place to visit – such as a site that has been built over – then it will be difficult for even keen visitors to imagine the scene of the battle and the site will not attract either visitors or the ever-increasing number of historical re-enactors. The site thus loses its historical and educational value.

Within easy reach of Greater London, but outside the immediate geographical range of this book, are two battle sites that should be experienced, because they provide a glimpse into a bloody part of English Civil War history and encapsulate, in a compact form, the best in exploring battlefield sites. The two are Old Basing House and St Lawrence's Church at nearby Alton. Both are in the immediate location of Basingstoke in Hampshire.

Basing House is now an English Heritage ruin situated just off the M3 at Old Basing near Basingstoke. The house, as well as its associated barn, was the scene of much bloody fighting between besieged Royalists and besieging Roundheads. In 1645, after periods of siege the Roundheads launched a final and successful attack on what had been one of the grandest, richest houses in the country, which belonged to the defiant Royalist the Marquis of Winchester. The final attack lasted less than 2 hours; the attackers drove the defenders back and a last stand was made at the gatehouse of the old house. Cromwell, who was present, allowed his troops to plunder the house, after which, probably by accident, it caught fire and burned. The additional tragedy here is that:

> Civilians as well as soldiers were killed in the assault, including six Catholic priests and one woman (after she protested at the treatment of her father who had been taken prisoner and was badly wounded). Between 100 and 200 defenders were killed; the rest taken prisoner, including the Marquis. Cromwell allowed his troops to plunder the riches of the house: money, plate, jewels, hangings, and furniture to the value of £200,000. Having been looted bare, Basing House itself caught fire, probably by accident; heated shot was fired against the house during the attack and it is possible that a small fire wasn't properly doused and had remained smoldering unperceived. Not all of the prisoners had been taken out of the house before the fire started, and those who were still locked in the vaults were left to burn to death.

The scars made by musket shot are still visible on the side of a barn, reminding us of the summary executions handed out to those men, women, and children who resisted the Parliamentary forces at the old house opposite.

Three hundred yards from the ruined house is the church of St Marys, which was occupied and desecrated by the Roundhead forces. It is well worth a visit, as one can see where the Roundheads fired from into the house.

The sixteenth-century Great Barn, the scene of some of the bloodiest fighting. Cannon damage is visible on the top right hand wall. (*Author*)

Nearby is the town of Alton, where in 1643 3,000 Parliamentarian troops attacked and caught by surprise the incumbent Royalists, who fell back in desperate fighting to the church of St Lawrence. They fought across the graveyard, leaving their dead scattered behind them as they took refuge in the church, where they piled dead horses against the door. Yet the Parliamentarians succeeded in gaining entry. Between 100 and 200 men died, and 900 more Royalists were taken prisoner. The Royalist leader Colonel Boles was shot and killed in the pulpit, which still remains. The church doors were pock marked with musket shot holes that can still be seen.

The prisoners were forced to bury their dead comrades in a grave along the north side of the church. The peaceful atmosphere within the church belies its stormy past.

As mentioned, battlefields are places where people died, and it is this unavoidable fact that adds to the poignancy of many of the sites. Evocative names on ancient maps remind us of the consequence of conflict: 'Bloody Meadow', 'Slaughter Field', 'Dead Man's Bottom', and the remains of mortuary chapels and churches where post-battle burial took place hint at the human dramas that took place usually over no more than three or four hours, and often changed the course of our history; that is if burial took place at all. It was common practice to leave one's enemy unburied even for years after the event. In the case of the First World War, plaques commemorate the sites of some of the worst disasters. These will be looked at in Chapter Nine.

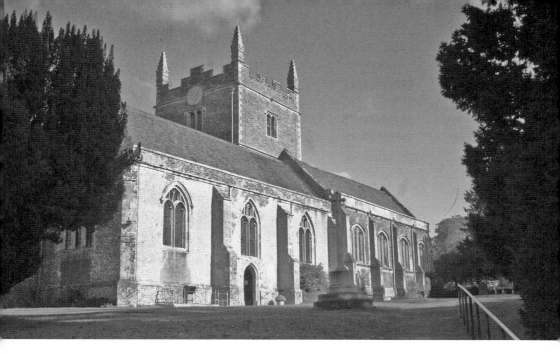

Above: St Mary's Church, Old Basing, where Cromwell lodged his men and stabled his horses. (*Author*)

Right: Three bullet holes can be seen in this small section of door alone. (*Author*)

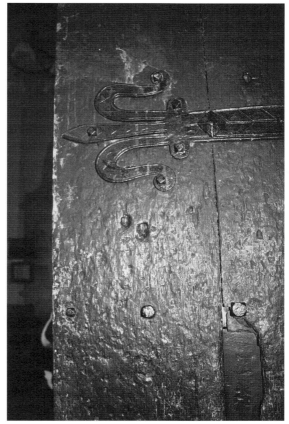

Pulpit where Colonel Boles was killed, and relics, including musket balls, retrieved during church renovation. (*Author*)

CHAPTER ONE

The Grim Reality of
Early Warfare

There is a tendency to think of early battles as having been fought to a code of honour and chivalry. Recent research and work on remains discovered on early battlefields show that in reality battlefields during and after the battle itself could be brutal beyond imagination.

Nature of Death

The most dangerous part of a battle was when it was clear that one side was winning, and the losing side turned to flee, exposing themselves to the pursuing party. In order to escape quickly, it was common practice to take off one's armour, throw away one's weapons, and run. This made the escaping soldiers particularly vulnerable when being hunted down by pursuing cavalry who tended to view fleeing enemy as fair sporting targets. There are numerous reports of post-battle events that expose the brutality of what normally followed. For example, after William's victory on the field at Hastings in 1066, a contemporary Norman account describes what happened when the English started to flee:

> ...And made off as soon as they got the chance, some on looted horses, many on foot; some along the roads, many across country. Those who struggled but on rising lacked the strength to flee lay in their own blood. The sheer will to survive gave strength to others. Many left their corpses in the depths of the forests, many collapsed in the path of their pursuers along the way. The Normans [...] pursued them keenly, slaughtering the guilty fugitives and bringing matters

to a fitting end, while the hooves of the horses exacted punishment from the dead as they were ridden over.[9]

Sean McGlynn, in his recent work dealing with 'the savage reality of the so-called "Age of Chivalry"', has selected a number of eye-witness accounts on medieval battlefields with a view to dispelling some of the myths. He quotes from an eyewitness account on the English side at Agincourt, who describes what happened once the English archers had finished firing into the French ranks and took up swords to finish off their opponents:

> Fear and trembling seized them, even of their more nobly born, who that day surrendered themselves more than ten times. No one, however, had time to take them prisoner, but almost all, without distinction of person, were as soon as they were struck down put to death without respite, either by those who had laid them low or by others following [...] So great was the undisciplined violence and pressure of the mass of men behind that the living fell on top of the dead, and others falling on top of the living were killed as well, with the result that in each of the three places where the strong contingents guarding our standards [was] such a great heap grew of the slain and those of the lying crushed in-between that our men climbed up those heaps, which had risen above a man's height, and butchered their enemies down below with swords, axes, and other weapons.[10]

Early warfare was as much about financial gain as righting perceived wrongs. A medieval knight who took to the battlefield and took an important prisoner could make a small fortune in ransom. After the battle and sometimes prematurely, as at Barnet 1471, there was the inducement of plunder; the reality, as will be shown, was a cold-blooded ruthlessness in the manner of fighting, the debilitating effect of the weapons used, and frequently, the lack of mercy shown. During the Wars of the Roses, of which three battles in and around London will be looked at, there were few hostage opportunities in what was a series of dynastic, gangster-style conflicts. The bitter family feuds led to the quarrelling nobility executing their defeated opponents and rivals, often in a savage manner, thus keeping alive the cycle of killing and revenge. Their enemies were safer despatched. A recent study has accumulated some statistics that make interesting observations on the brutality of medieval warfare: between 1455 and 1471 there was an increasing number of executions of the nobility, culminating with the Battle of Wakefield, 'When these executions became commonplace [...] chivalry, a troubled and romanticised concept from its inception, no longer existed even between those of the highest rank.'[11]

Reconstructing events on the battlefield can be difficult. The number of chroniclers who had first-hand military experience of any kind was small.'[12] We can, however, through the study of the remains of combatants determine the way battles were fought and the effects of the weaponry.

Grim Reality

There are really only two sites in Europe that have been uncovered in the last century that allow us an insight into the cruel nature of early warfare. The first is a series of burial pits from the Battle of Visby, a Hanseatic city in Sweden, which was fought in 1361 on the island of Gotland between the Danish King and the Gotland peasants. The Danes were victorious. Five mass-graves were located outside the Visby city's walls. The initial discovery was made in 1905, and at least three more were located up to 1928. It was customary for the victors to strip the losers of anything of value, including armour and weapons, then make sure they were despatched before the corpses were flung into a pit. Over 1,185 human remains were found, and many more were inaccessible due to being obstructed by the city walls. Examination of the corpses, some of which still had their armour showed a total of 456 wounds made by cutting weapons. 126 were piercing wounds from arrows, lances, and wooden balls studded with metal spikes attached to a short handle that had a chain; these were used against the head and shoulders from horseback. There was also much evidence of use of the mace and war hammer, characterised by smashed skulls and square-shaped holes in skulls respectively. The war hammer was often used to finish off a dying opponent. Cutting wounds were much in evidence, with one horrific example showing that a single sword blow aimed at the upper legs had severed both legs, cleanly and simultaneously. The skull on page 21 has led to speculation as to the sequence of events that killed him. It has been suggested that:

> Two quick hammer blows to fell [him] and the arrows landing after, or a hail of arrows which he had turned his back on, and then later two hammer blows to put him out of his misery. Before stripping and dumping him with his mates. The grouping of the arrow heads is particularly spectacular and it makes one wonder if they used the tactic of a hail of arrows, as in the later Battle of Crecy, where it is said the English longbow men kept 100,000 arrows in the air at one time.[13]

Graves have been excavated in modern times to bring clarification in the events. It showed that at least one-third of the Gotlandian army consisted of minors and elderly. Many of the dead defenders were unusually buried in their armour because, according to historian John Keegan:

> ...Hot weather and their great number (about 2,000 bodies were disinterred 600 years later) defeated the efforts of the victors to strip them before

decomposition began. The site of the excavation yielded one of the most fearsome revelations of a medieval battle known to archaeologists.

The only mass graves of known medieval battle victims to have been found in England were those of the Battle of Towton, which was fought near Tadcaster in South Yorkshire on 29 March 1461 between Edward of York (King Edward IV) and the mentally unstable Lancastrian Henry VI. The Visby find of 1,185 individuals from four separate pits was far larger than the find at Towton Hall, a residence about 1 mile from the battlefield. Towton is regarded as the bloodiest battle to ever take place on English soil, and evidence from forty-three, mostly-complete individuals discovered in a grave during building work at Towton Hall in August 1996 has allowed insight into the way the battle was fought. The University of Bradford Biological Anthropology Research Centre states:

> Many of the individuals suffered multiple injuries that are far in excess of those necessary to cause disability and death. From the distribution of cuts, chops, incisions, and punctures, it appears that blows cluster in the craniofacial area, in some cases bisecting the face and cranial vault of some individuals and detaching bone in others. Series of cuts and incisions found in the vicinity of the nasal and aural areas appear to have been directed toward removal of the nose and ears. There are few infra-cranial (torso and limb) injuries, which may suggest that these areas were not targeted, that these individuals were wearing armour, or that they sustained their injuries while in a position that did not allow them to defend themselves. The pattern, distribution, and number of these insults argues for perimortem mutilation. Many were left in a state that would have made identification difficult, even more so as they had been stripped of identifiable weapons and clothing prior to interment (a normal practice in the medieval period).

It is likely that around 28,000 men were killed.[14] The skull illustrated below with damage to front and back is that of a male, between thirty-six and forty-five years old. The brutality of his death has been deciphered by the structure of the fractures on his skull:

> The precise order can be worked out from the direction of fractures on his skull: when bone breaks, the cracks veer towards existing areas of weakness. The first five blows were delivered by a bladed weapon to the left-hand side of his head, presumably by a right-handed opponent standing in front of him. None is likely to have been lethal. The next one almost certainly was. From behind him someone swung a blade towards his skull, carving a down-to-up trajectory through the air. The blow opened a huge horizontal gash into the back of his head – picture a slit you could post an envelope through. Fractures

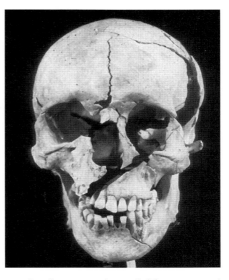

Above: Skull from the mass grave uncovered in Visby on the Island of Gotland.

Right: Sharp force trauma across the face.

Below: This skull is unusual in that it was recovered still wearing the coife. This is unusual because it was normal for the fallen to be stripped of all weapons, armour, and clothing before burial, if burial took place at all.

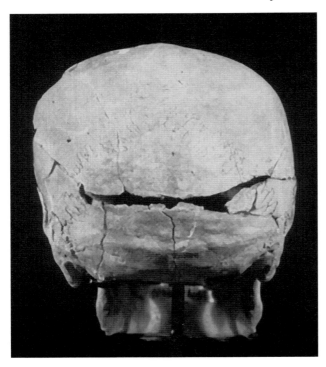

Close up of blunt force trauma, showing radiating fractures.

raced down to the base of his skull and around the sides of his head. Fragments of bone were forced in to [the] brain, felling him. His enemies were not done yet. Another small blow to the right and back of the head may have been enough to turn him over onto his back. Finally, another blade arced towards him. This one bisected his face, opening a crevice that ran from his left eye to his right jaw [see picture]. It cut deep; the edge of the blade reached to the back of his throat.[15]

From the burial pit uncovered at Towton, there were seventy-three wounds on twenty-eight crania, twelve of which were puncture wounds. A number of arrowheads were found in the pit, and one burial had an arrow embedded in a vertebrae. At least two burials had their noses removed by sharp weapons, and many skulls had numerous cuts bisecting the face. Some had the top of the cranium almost removed by the force of a blow. Healed fractures on some of the skull are an indication that they had probably fought elsewhere.

CHAPTER TWO

The Dim and Distant Past: The Boudicca Rebellion AD 61, the Sack of London and the 'Battle of Watling Street'

As mentioned in the introduction, nearly all of our knowledge of Boudicca and her rebellion come from a couple of pages written by the Roman historian Tacitus (AD 56-117). He was a senator and a historian, who because of his position and relationship to the Roman General Agricola, who fought in Britain, is generally regarded as being a reliable source.[16] He mentions Boudicca in both *The Agricola* and *The Annals of Imperial Rome*. Agricola was his father-in-law, who served with the military governor of Britain at the time of the revolt. There is little reason to doubt the fundamental facts relating to the nature of the rebellion and its consequences. There is a later account (*c.* AD 164 -235) by the Greek-Roman historian Cassius Dio, but outside of archaeology, had the accounts written by Tacitus and Dio not survived, we would never have even heard of Boudicca. We have only the Dio account as to her physical appearance, which has inspired much Victorian and modern portraiture, but again it is written over a century and a half after her demise and its accuracy must be viewed with suspicion. For the final battle, Tacitus informs us that Boudicca poisoned herself after her defeat, and Dio states that she became ill and died. There could be a link between the two.

It is through Tacitus in the *Annals* that we have the names of the three key towns destroyed, Camulodunum, (Colchester), Londinium, (London), and Verulamium (St Albans). Archaeological excavation within London,[17] shows that destruction by fire took place at around the appropriate time of AD 60/61, and the desecration of a number of graves can be attributed to the same period, but without the scanty early written records Boudicca would be a nameless and faceless ghost of the past, whose existence would have long disappeared into the mists of time.[18]

For the fate of London, Tacitus tells us that London was 'a place not dignified with the name of a colony, but the chief residence of merchants, and the great mart of trade and commerce'. Therefore, Tacitus tells us, the Roman Governor Suetonius decided that London was not the most effective place to wait for and destroy the rampaging Boudicca. He decided to leave London to its fate:

...He [Suetonius] resolved to quit the station, and by giving up one post, secure the rest of the province. Neither supplications nor the tears of the inhabitants could induce him to change his plan. The signal for the march was given. All who chose to follow his banners were taken under his protection. Of all whom, on account of their advanced age, the weakness of their sex, or the attractions of the situation thought proper to remain behind, not one escaped the rage of the Barbarians. The inhabitants of Verulamium, a municipal town, were in like manner put to the sword. The genius of a savage people leads them always in quest of plunder, and accordingly, the Britons left behind them all places of strength. Wherever they expected feeble resistance and considerable booty, there they were sure to attack with the fiercest rage. Military skill was not the talent of Barbarians. The number massacred in the places which have been mentioned amounted to no less than 70,000, all citizens or allies of Rome. To make prisoners and reserve them for slavery or to exchange them was not in the idea of a people who despised all the laws of war. The halter and the gibbet, slaughter and defoliation, fire and sword were the marks of savage valour. Aware that vengeance would overtake them, they were resolved to make sure of their revenge, and glut themselves with the blood of their enemies.[19]

The Final Battle

Tacitus left us a description of the place for the final battle, which has almost limitless possibilities. Just some of the suggested sites for the battle range from the area of King's Cross, Parliament Hill Fields in Hampstead, to Mancetter, which has now become part of Atherstone in Warwickshire, and is the site of a Roman settlement.[20]

A nineteenth century history of London makes reference to an area called Battle Bridge, where Kings Cross now stands:

Battle Bridge is so called for two reasons. In the first place, there was formerly a small brick bridge over the Fleet at this spot; and secondly because, as London tradition has steadily affirmed, here was fought the great battle between Suetonius Paulinus, the Roman general, and Boadicea, the Queen of the Iceni. It is still doubtful whether the scene of the great battle was so near London, but there is still much to be said in its favour. The arguments pro and con are

An idealised version of Queen Boudicca.

worth a brief discussion. Tacitus describes the spot, with his usual sharp, clear brevity: 'Suetonius,' he says, 'chose a place with narrow jaws, backed by a forest.' Now the valley of the Fleet, between Pentonville and Gray's Inn Lane, backed by the great northern forest of Middlesex, undoubtedly corresponds with this description, but then Tacitus, always clear and vivid, makes no mention of the River Fleet, which would have been most important as a defence for the front and flank of the Roman army, and this raises up serious doubts. The Roman summer camp near Barnsbury Park, opposite Minerva Terrace, in the Thornhill Road, we have already mentioned. There was a praetorium there, a raised breastwork, long visible from the Caledonian Road, a well, and a trench. In 1825, arrow-heads and red-tiled pavements were discovered in this spot.

The author continues by mentioning:

In 1842, a fragment of a Roman monumental inscription was found built into a cottage on the east side of Maiden Lane. It was part of the tomb of an officer of the twentieth legion, which had been dug up in a field on the west side of the road leading to the Caledonian Asylum. This legion formed part of the army of Claudius, which Paulinus led against Boadicea.[21]

Another, more recent history, *A Survey of London* (1952), observes:

There is no foundation for the stories of a battle here between the Romans and the Britons. The only Roman find discovered near Battle Bridge is the fragment of a tombstone to the memory of 'Saturninus, private in the Twentieth Valerian Victorious Legion', found on the eastern side of Maiden Lane in 1842. The neighbourhood was generally known as Battle Bridge until the erection of King's Cross [a memorial to George IV] in 1830, when the latter name superseded it. But the name of Battle Bridge was attached not only to the hamlet near the ancient bridge and specifically to the houses.[22]

Martin Marix Evans, an expert in the field of the Boudiccan revolt, has produced a well-reasoned article that puts the likelihood of the battle on the A5, Roman Watling Street, at Cuttle Mill in the immediate vicinity of Towcester, the former Roman town of Lactodorum. Marix Evans' argument runs as follows:

The Roman road still runs past Cuttle Mill. Driving north on the A5 from Milton Keynes [...] it follows the line of Roman Watling Street closely [...] A length of the agger, the embankment which carried the Roman road, is still to be seen in line with the road on the far horizon when looking south from the public footpath that strikes west halfway up the hill. To the north, on the top of the ridge, a road heads north-east from the A5 towards Shutlanger and Stoke Bruerne through the tiny hamlet of Heathencote, from which a public footpath runs east, descending on to the plain before climbing again to Alderton. Alderton stands on the southern ridge, along which a north-east to south-west road goes to connect it to Paulerspury. From Alderton, the public footpath to Heathencote joins another path that follows the stream coming from Cuttle Mill back to the A5 on the bridge and embankment above the water. The whole area can thus be explored on public footpaths [...] From Suetonius' point of view it is perfect. The rear of his force is in contact with the road to Towcester and possible reinforcements from Bicester (Alchester) coming along Akeman Street. To the south, Watling Street passes through the Whittlewood Forest, which occupies all the higher ground west of the Tove valley, and so the cavalry can prevent any attempt to outflank him there. The northern flank is protected by the Heathencote spur, which today furnishes visitors to Towcester races with such a fine view of the course. The spot height on the summit over which Watling Street passes near here is 121 m (397 feet) and the spot height at the crossroads with the Alderton-Paulerspury road is 114 m (374 feet).

Paulerspury lies on the ridge behind the church. Cuttle Mill and Watling Street lie to the left of the picture. (*Author*)

Cuttle Mill, situated 300 yards from the A5, Watling Street. (*Author*)

Burial of the Dead

There has been a persistent belief that Boudicca is buried under Platform Ten of King's Cross Station. This is possibly an extension of the idea that the final battle took place in the area. Alternatively, it originates from a book written by Lewis Spence in 1937. There is no reason whatsoever to believe that she lies buried here. We know from Tacitus that Boudicca fled from the battlefield, but to date the site of the final battle is uncertain. On the basis that Suetonius says he abandoned London to its fate, the likelihood is that the battle took place in the vicinity of one of the major Roman roads out of London. Another suggested place of burial is Parliament Hill in Highgate, where there is what would appear to be an ancient burial mound, now surrounded by rails. Following a dig carried out in 1894 by Sir Hercules Read, no human bones were found, but plenty of eighteenth century rubbish was.[23]

Excavations in the City of London have uncovered possible evidence of the desecration of Roman graves by Boudicca's forces when London was sacked and burned in AD 60/61.

> Archaeologists from Wessex Archaeology found a small cremation cemetery from London's earliest years that had been severely disturbed some time before the 1970s – the date is given by a coin overlying the site [...] Contemporary with the cremation cemetery, the partly-decomposed body of a middle-aged or elderly man had been thrown into an open drainage ditch, with the partly-decayed head of a young woman placed between his legs. The bodies were left uncovered. The man's skeleton was missing its lower legs, while the woman's skull had lost its jawbone [...] 'It is hard not to associate this with Boudicca's sack of London, as the dates match,' said project director Chris Moore. Once London was reoccupied after Boudicca's revolt, the site was rebuilt as two properties – a group of industrial buildings and a large timber-framed shop in the late first century, replaced by two high-status masonry town houses from the mid-second century. These went out of use in the third century, but survived to provide building stone until the eleventh or twelfth centuries.[24]

Until recently, the Museum of London held a series of skulls that had been put forward as likely victims of the revolt, but in a communication with the author Jenny Hall, the curator of the Roman London collections says:

> We no longer think that the disarticulated skulls that have been found in the Walbrook stream or the Thames are associated with the Boudiccan destruction. Recent excavations of part of a Roman cemetery just north of the city wall have found that many of the burials, sited on the banks of the Walbrook stream and other channels, were eroded by the water courses, with bones being washed

The tumulus where legend has it Boudicca was buried. No evidence for this has ever been uncovered. (*Author*)

into the stream. Skulls would travel down the stream more easily than other bones and became lodged in the lower courses. When found previously, with a large degree of historic licence, we said that some may have been victims of the Boudiccan massacre. Now we have the evidence from this cemetery, we no longer believe this to be the case.

She continues by observing, as previously mentioned, that apart from the destruction by fire of the town there is little evidence for the Boudiccan revolt, and as yet, no definite victims of the massacre.

CHAPTER THREE

The Peasants' Revolt, 1381

Part of John Ball's speech to the rebels at Blackheath: 'When Adam delved and Eve span, who was then the gentleman?'

Background

The Peasants' Revolt of 1381, of which London was the key focus of the rebels, began in Brentwood Essex as a reaction to an over-zealous poll-tax collector. The King was the fourteen-year-old boy Richard II, the ruler of an all but bankrupt country, ineffectively at war with France, and effectively in the hands of his unpopular uncle John of Gaunt, the Duke of Lancaster. The labour shortage created by the Black Death of 1349 highlighted underlying grievances relating to serfdom. Workers now had greater power, and the revolt soon spread to neighbouring counties. Hertfordshire, Kent, Norfolk, and Suffolk rose first. Destruction and looting was widespread. The revolt, triggered by insensitive poll-tax collectors and the iniquities in the poll-tax system, was widely recorded at the time, such was the fear it instilled in the governing classes. The whole rebellion from beginning to end scarcely lasted a month, but the scars left on London in particular ran deep. The rioters pillaged and murdered at random, and the path they took can still be followed. It takes in a number of major London landmarks. The leaders of the revolt were John Ball, Wat Tyler, and Jack Straw, all of whom were ultimately captured and executed.

Sources

We have many contemporary and early sources that tell the events of what has been designated the 'Summer of Blood'. Many can be accessed directly on the internet. Probably the best source for events in London is the *Anonimalle Chronicle*. The identity of the author is unknown, but he would appear to have had access to the royal court.[25] Thomas Walsingham's *The St Albans Chronicle* (1376-1394). Henry Knighton's *The Westminster Chronicle* (1381-1394) deals with the revolt in London. Jean Froissart (*c*. 1337-1405), who has been described as 'inventive',[26] and was also close to the royal court, is regarded as a good source if treated with care. His work *Chronicles* (Book II) deals with the events in England and France during the period 1376-1385.

Places Involved in the Uprising

This battlefield begins with the arrival of between 50,000 and 60,000 rebels at Blackheath Hill, leads through Southwark, over London Bridge and back to the Tower of London, St Katherine's Dock, Tower Hill, and into the City of London. It finishes at Smithfield with the Mayor of London, William Walworth, stabbing Wat Tyler, and Tyler being carried into St Bartholomew's Church in Smithfield, before being dragged out and decapitated.

Negotiation

On 6 June, Richard II said he would come and listen to what the rebels had to say, and would meet them 'on the shore below Blackheath'. The rebels had taken the constable of Rochester Castle Sir John Newton as a hostage to be used in communicating with the King. As the rebels approached London, coming from Blackheath via Southwark on 12 June 1381, the drawbridge in the middle of London Bridge was raised and the city gates were closed.

Froissart tells us that in order to arrange the meeting Newton came by boat, as instructed by the rebels, to the tower, where he was welcomed by the King and his attending nobles and dignitaries, who were anxious for news:

> This knight Sir John Newton, who was well known among them, for he was one of the King's officers, kneeled down before the King and said: 'My right redoubted Lord, let it not displease your grace the message that I must needs shew you, for dear sir, it is by force and against my will.'
>
> 'Sir John,' said the King, 'say what ye will; I hold you excused.'

Rochester Castle, London Road, captured by the rebels in 1381, and Sir John Newton, captured as a hostage to be used in communicating with the King. (*Author*)

'Sir, the commons of this your realm hath sent me to you to desire you to come and speak with them on Blackheath, for they desire to have none but you. And, Sir, ye need not to have any doubt of your person, for they will do you no hurt, for they hold and will hold you for their King. But Sir, they say they will shew you divers things, the which shall be right necessary for you to take heed of, when they speak with you; of the which things, sir, I have no charge to shew you. But, Sir, it may please you to give me an answer such as may appease them and that they may know for truth that I have spoken with you, for they have my children in hostage till I return again to them, and without I return again, they will slay my children incontinent.'

Then the king made him an answer and said, 'Sir, ye shall have an answer shortly.' Then the King took counsel what was best for him to do, and it was anon determined that the next morning the King should go down the river by water and without fail to speak with them. And when Sir John Newton heard that answer he desired nothing else and so took his leave of the King and of the lords and returned again into his vessel, and passed the Thames and went to Blackheath, where he had left more than threescore thousand men. And there he answered them that the next morning they should send some of their council to the Thames, and there the King would come and speak with them.[27]

The expansive view over London from Blackheath Common. (*Author*)

Wat Tyler Road on Blackheath commemorates the rebel encampment. (*Author*)

The scene on Blackheath on the night of 12/13 June has been described by Dan Jones:[28]

> ...The crackle and glow of campfires would have lined the heath, casting an eerie, wavering light over excited, dirty faces, filled with pride and expectation. An incredible adventure was about to reach its climax before the highest, most worshipful authority [the King] of all. The fires may just have appeared as tiny orange pinpricks in the night, visible from the Tower upriver, where a young king slept, preparing for the first great showdown of his life [...] The City of London on 13 June was celebrating Corpus Christi and was buzzing with strangers. There were rebels mainly from Essex now camped in fields near Mile End, a few miles up the Aldgate Road, a road whose entrance to the city was just 1,500 yards north of the Tower [... the] Kent rebels amassed down river in Greenwich, camped on Blackheath Hill...[29]

The following day, the King heard mass, probably at the tower chapel, and he and a train of four barges containing members of his court was 'rowed down along the Thames to Rotherhithe, 'Whereas was descended down the hill 10,000 men to see the King and to speak with him. And when they saw the King's barge coming they began to shout, and made such a cry as though all the devils of hell had been among them.'[30] Simon of Sudbury, Archbishop of Canterbury, and Sir Robert Hales, Royal Treasurer and prior of the Hospital of St. John's, both sitting next to the King, began to lose their nerve and suggested he should return to the tower. The King remained on his barge while a rebel brought to him by water a schedule of demands, which included the request that those around the King who had led him 'astray' be executed. These included the King's uncle John of Gaunt, Simon of Sudbury, Robert Hales, and others they blamed for their situation. Any thought of going ashore was for obvious reasons now abandoned. The barges returned to the tower and the rebels returned to Blackheath Hill, angered and planning vengeance.

The Violence Begins

Froissart tells us that the cry, 'Let us go to London,' went up. From Blackheath, there was only one route into London, and that was via Southwark and over London Bridge, which at that time had a drawbridge and was lined with buildings at the Southwark end. The rebels had sympathisers in the city, mainly motivated by a hatred of John of Gaunt, who had extensive property interests in London. Southwark was the first to suffer, particularly a brothel owned and rented from the mayor: '...They made for a brothel tucked away on the banks of the Southwark fishponds in a house rented from Mayor Walworth. They tore it down and set fire to it, terrifying the Flemish prostitutes inside and delighting those in the city proper who disapproved of the squalid tenement...'[31]

Froissart tells us:

>...At the bridge foot they [the rebels] threat them of London because the gates of the bridge were closed, saying how they would bren (burn) all the suburbs and so conquer London by force, and to slay and bren all the commons of the city. There were many within the city of their accord, and so they drew together and said, 'Why do we not let these good people enter into the city? They are your fellows, and that that they do is for us.' So therewith the gates were opened, and then these people entered into the city and went into houses and sat down to eat and drink...

Jones sums up:

>In a manner easy to follow in modern day London, the route followed by the rebels once they crossed over the former bridge [see illustration on p. 2] which came into the north bank at the Church of St Magnus the Martyr. The Church still stands, although rebuilt after the great fire of 1666. The City mob ahead of the incoming rebels [...] gathered and set out [...] for the western gates of London's wall [...] the Ludgate opened into Fleet Street, which in turn became the Strand. These were the main streets of medieval suburbia [...] The Londoners piled through the Ludgate and into this well-to-do neighbourhood.[32]

Obnoxious Legals: Sacking of the Temple

Sir Charles Oman, in his powerful early twentieth century history of the uprising *The Great Revolt*, tells us that by afternoon the insurgents turned their attention to the Temple, which was the legal headquarters for England:

>Here were their schools, and their library. Of all classes obnoxious to the insurgents, the legal profession was the most hated; it was they who were the tools of the manorial lords in binding the chains of the serfs [...] They burst into the church and there broke open the chests full of books, which they tore up and burnt in the street [...] 'It was marvellous to see,' says one chronicler, 'how even the most aged and infirm of them scrambled off with the agility of rats or evil spirits.'

The attack on the Temple church and the destruction of the documents therein was an attack by the mob on the legal system that they saw as failing to give them justice. From the Temple, the crowd continued along Fleet Street into the Strand, passing the assorted bishop's inns, St Mary le Strand, and other ecclesiastical buildings that had associations with the hated John of Gaunt. There was some plundering en route, but the main target was the absent John of Gaunt's palace, the Savoy, regarded as the finest residence in England.

An Evening at the Savoy

On 13 June, the rebels targeted the Savoy. It stood where the hotel of the same name stands today. Gaunt was occupied in Scotland. It was newly completed and full of valuables, including gifts from his father Edward III. The rebels first took food from the unfortunate citizens of London, and then running down the Strand shouted, 'To the Savoy.'[33] Servants aware of the situation ran towards the village of Charing, taking whatever they could carry. Oman describes what happened:[34]

> It was about four o'clock in the afternoon when the mob, swollen by thousands of apprentices, artisans, labourers, and professional criminals of the city, reached their goal. They went very methodically to work, the leaders repeatedly reminding them that they were come to destroy, not to steal; they were executing vengeance, not seeking profit. The doors of the palace were broken open, the caretakers having fled without offering resistance. Everything in the Savoy capable of destruction was then destroyed. The furniture was thrown out of the windows, and hacked to pieces in the street; the rich hangings, the clothes, and carpets were torn up; the plate and ornaments were broken into small fragments and cast into the river; the jewels, it is said, were smashed with hammers or brayed in a mortar. When the whole dwelling had been gutted it was set on fire and burnt to the ground. Its destruction was completed by the explosion of three barrels of gunpowder from the duke's armoury [...] A party of reprobates made their way to the cellars and there swilled the rich wines until they were overcome with bestial intoxication; they could not escape when the palace was fired, and so were smothered or burnt...

Tyler looked to destruction, not plunder, to make his point. When one rebel was spotted putting a silver goblet in his pocket, 'He was grabbed and hurled into the flames for violating Tyler's strict instructions not to turn a symbolic event into a thief's paradise. As the pilferer burnt to death, a stark warning was issued to the rest of the crowd – anyone else caught stealing would suffer the same fate.'[35] As the flames took hold, three barrels that the rebels thought contained precious metals were thrown onto the fire. Unfortunately for them, it contained gunpowder. The subsequent explosion led to large chunks of stone crashing down and trapping thirty rebels who were making merry in Gaunt's wine cellar. There they remained underground, and could be heard by passers-by, but no help was forthcoming. After seven days, they either starved or suffocated to death.[36] A contemporary report goes into more detail as to the fate of those rebels trapped by fire and falling masonry in the Savoy:[37]

> ...They could not crawl out, but passed their time with songs and catches, and other drunken inanities, until the door was blocked by fire and fallen stones, so that they could not have escaped if they had been sober, and there they remained until they died. For seven days afterwards, their cries and lamentations for the enormity of their sins were heard by many who went to that place, but there was none among their friends who helped or consoled them. And so they fuddled themselves with wine, having come to drink wine, and in wine they perished. It was reckoned afterwards that there was some thirty-two of them.

With the Savoy in flames, the rebels moved on; one part headed for Charing and Westminster, another group headed for Newgate to free its prisoners. The

The Savoy Hotel in the Strand, looking towards the Thames, occupies the site of John of Gaunt's Palace and the subsequent hospital. The Savoy Chapel was destroyed in 1381. There is still a chapel to be seen, but it dates from the 1490s, when rebuilding commenced. (*Author*)

mob was growing in strength. Knighton tells us that apprentices murdered their masters by beheading, because 'that was the only manner of death dealt out'.[38]

Execution of Roger Legett

There were eighteen executions in London that evening. The best-known victim was a 'quest-monger' [lawyer] named Roger Legett. Legett stood for everything that the rebels loathed:

> For years he had profited from dispensing partial justice and conniving with colleagues, like the undersheriff of London John Butterwick, to obstruct, delay, or deny due process of law and therefore the true and dutiful governance of England. He showed little concern for the life or limb of those who crossed him.[39]

Legett, aware that he was being hunted, fled to St Martin le Grand, no longer standing, which was famous for offering sanctuary.

The rebels burst into the chapel and dragged Legett down West Cheap to Cheapside, where 'at the confluence of Milk Street, Wood Street, and Bread Street, they stopped. This was a well-known place of trade, conversation, preaching, water-gathering, and public punishment. Legett was pushed to the ground.'[40] He was beheaded in front of the Eleanor Cross. The mob then moved on to the Priory of St John of Jerusalem in Clerkenwell, of which the hated Sir Robert Hales was the prior.

The only remaining sections of the twelfth century priory are St John's Gate and the crypt of St John's in Clerkenwell. It was the home of the Knights Hospitaller, an order of crusading knights in Clerkenwell, near Smithfield. As the mob passed through Holborn, they destroyed all properties that had belonged to Legett and the priory. So complete was the destruction of the priory that it burned for a week.

By the end of a day of destruction, the mob camped on Tower Hill and in the Hospital of St Katherine, at what is today St Katherine's Marina. The area would have glowed with bonfires. The King and his court were now effectively blocked into the tower with a guard of around 1,200 men. The rebels were demanding the surrender of their enemies

Richard II undoubtedly had no choice but to negotiate or see the tower destroyed. Accordingly, he sent a messenger with a letter to the mob at St Katherine's Wharf, asking them to set out their grievances, and then in return for a pardon they were to take themselves home. The rebels, heady with their recent successes, refused. The King was asked to hand over Archbishop Sudbury and Treasurer Hales. The King was particularly close to Sudbury and he sought

Details from the 1562 Agas map of London showing the Eleanor Cross where it meets Wood Street. It was near here, in sight of the Eleanor Cross, that many of the victims of the rebels were beheaded. Wood Street still remains. The tower of Bow Church can be seen bottom right opposite Honey Lane, the site of the 'Standard'.

Cheapside: the first alley on the right is Honey Lane, opposite where the 'Standard' stood. Just over the road is Bow Church. It was here that executions took place, including those carried out by Wat Tyler, and later Jack Cade. (*Author*)

Left: View of the procession of Marie de Medici along Cheapside, City of London, 1638 (1809). The Queen's entourage passing the Eleanor Cross and the Little Conduit on Cheapside, as seen from Friday Street. Although dated 1809, this illustration gives a good idea of the layout of Cheapside as seen from the 'Standard'. It was here that the rebels executed their victims.

Below: So complete was the destruction that the priory burned for a week. The gatehouse in the centre of the picture still remains.

another solution. This time, he sent two knights over to St Katharine's, offering pardons in return for going home.

The rebels saw this as a dismissal. An angry mob stormed into London. At 7 a.m. the following morning, the King and a small party (some of which, through fear, deserted him) went to meet the rebels at Mile End. He handled the situation well, remaining calm, pacifying the rebels, and offering them a solution to their grievances. He did, however, make one fatal mistake: he agreed to the rebels' demand that they could hunt down and deal with those whom they saw as traitors to their sovereign, and deal with them themselves, i.e. 'lawfully.' What this really meant was that the rebels had carte blanche to hunt down and kill all those that they regarded as their enemies, and on the face of it stay within the law. This is precisely what they proceeded to do. It was while the King was at Mile End that Tyler, Ball, Straw, and a party of rebels made a dash for the tower.

The Storming of the Tower

The drawbridge was left down, possibly due to the belief of those on guard (180 or so archers) that to raise it would infuriate the rebels and endanger the absent King's life. Alternatively, the guard that remained lost its nerve at the taunting coming across the moat from the rebels camped on Tower Hill. The sight of smoke from burning buildings and the very real possibility that the rebels would succeed must have contributed to the decision to lower the drawbridge. No doubt the hope among the royal party was that Sudbury, Hales, and other targets of the rebels would be able to quietly slip away while the King, heading out to Mile End, acted as a distraction for the rebels. But the rebel leaders saw this as precisely the best opportunity to make their entry into the tower.

Stow, in the 1603 edition of his work on London, tells us:

> In the yeare 1381, the Rebels of Kent drew out of the tower (where the King was then lodged) Simon Sudberie, Archbishop of Canterburie, Lord Chancellor, Robert Hales, Prior of S. Iohns, and Treasurer of England, William Appleton Frier, the King's confessor, and Iohn Legge, a sargeant of the kings, and beheaded them on the Tower hill, &c...[41]

Neither Archbishop Sudbury nor Treasurer Sir Robert Hales could be described as deserving of their fates, or even particularly responsible for the rebels' grievances. They were both aware of what their fates would be if captured. They were now dragged out of the chapel of the tower while praying. On Friday 14 June, while Richard and his entourage were meeting the rebels at Mile End, Oman tells us:

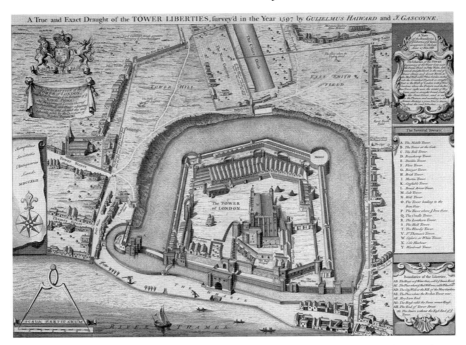

This early map of London, *c.* 1562, gives us an idea of the aspects of Tower Hill (top left) and St Katherine's (to the right of the tower complex). (*Agas*)

...The murderers burst in [...] there was a general howl of triumph – the traitor, the spoiler of the people, was run to earth. Sudbury boldly stood forward and faced the horde: 'Here am I, your Archbishop ... no traitor nor spoiler am I.' But the insurgents rushed in upon him, cruelly buffeted him, and dragged him out of the chapel and across the courts of the Tower to the hill outside, where they beheaded him upon a log of wood. The headsman's work was so badly done that eight strokes were spent in hacking through the unhappy prelate's neck. His companion, the treasurer Hales, was executed immediately after...

Dan Jones elaborates on Sudbury's final moments on Tower Hill:

Onlookers had heard him cry out that this was the hand of God, and when the second blow had fallen, he had instinctively raised his fingers to touch the [first] wound. The executioner, excited but hopelessly inaccurate, had chopped off the ends of his ringed fingers. Now the bloodied head sat on top of a pole; above, the *coup de grace* – Sudbury's red mitre nailed on his skull.[42]

Froissart tells us that while in the tower searching out Sudbury and Hales the King's mother was abused by the rebels:

St John's Gate from Clerkenwell Road. (*Author*)

East side of White Tower overlooking St Katherine's. From one of the towers, the fourteen-year-old Richard II observed the camped rebels on Tower Hill and St Katherine's wharf. (*Author*)

The young King Richard II sets out to meet the rebels at Rotherhythe (from Jean Froissart's *Chronicles*). Fifteenth-century manuscript of Richard II meeting with the rebels of the 1381 Peasants' Revolt.

These gluttons entered into the princess' chamber and brake her bed, whereby she was so sore affrayed that she swooned; and there she was taken up and borne to the water side and put into a barge and covered, and so conveyed to a place called the Queen's Wardrobe; [a palace near Blackfriars] and there she was all that day and night like a woman half dead, till she was comforted with the King her son, as ye shall hear after.

One lucky escapee was the young Earl of Derby, the future King Henry IV, who was hidden by a loyal soldier in a cupboard. This was an act of kindness that Derby, as King, rewarded many years later.

Illustration of how the tower and the drawbridge would have appeared to the rebels in 1381. (*Author*)

Western entrance, 2011. It was here that the rebels intimidated the guards and persuaded them to allow entry. (*Author*)

Plunder in the City

The rebels dragged their victims to a convenient and well-established point of execution in Cheapside known as the 'standard', which was located opposite Honey Lane within yards of St Mary le Bow Church. Stowe, in his 1603 *Survey of London*, tells us:[43]

> Of executions at the Standard in Cheape, we read that in the yeare 1293 three men had their right hands smitten off there for rescuing of a prisoner arrested by an officer of the citie. In the yeare 1326, the Burgesses of London caused Walter Stapleton, bishop of Excester, treasurer to Edward the 2nd, and other, to be beheaded at the Standard in Cheape (but this was by Paul's gate). In the yere 1351, the 26 of Ed[ward] the 3rd, two Fishmongers were beheaded at the standard in Cheape, but I read not of their offence. 1381. Wat Tiler beheaded Richard Lions, and other there. In the yere 1399, H[enry] the 4th caused the blanch Charters made by Ri[chard] the 2nd to be burnt there. In the yeare 1450, Iacke Cade captaine of the Kentish Rebels, beheaded the Lord Say there. In the yere 1461, Iohn Davy had his hand stricken off there, because he had stricken a man before the Iudges at Westminster, &c.

Here on Tower Hill, Simon of Sudbury and Sir Robert Hales were executed by the mob. They had the dubious honour of being the first recorded to die on Tower Hill. (*Author*)

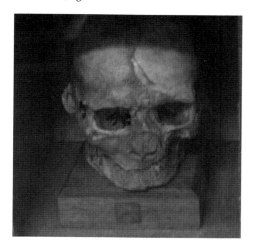

Simon of Sudbury's partially mummified head can be viewed in a glass case at St Gregory's Church, Sudbury, Suffolk. The rest of his body is buried in a tomb near the Black Prince in Canterbury Cathedral. (*Author*)

The rebels, in a mixture of xenophobia and a belief that they were responsible for the running of London's brothels, had singled out foreigners, many of them Flemings, for particularly harsh treatment. Most of them had their homes clustered around the churches of St James Garlickhithe and St Martin-in-the-Vintry:[44]

> Some 150 or 160 unhappy foreigners were murdered in various places – 35 Flemings in one batch were dragged out of the church of St Martin in the Vintry, and beheaded on the same block [...] Disorderly bands [...] went about putting to passers-by the watch-word 'with whom hold you?' and if the person interrogated refused to say 'with King Richard and the true commons' they tore of his hood and raised the hue and cry upon him, and dragged him to one of the blocks, which they had set up on street corners, to be beheaded. It is recorded that they killed no one save by the axe, and that the larger proportion of the victims were either lawyers, jurymen of the city, persons connected with the levying of taxes, or known adherents of the Duke of Lancaster.[45]

The Friday and Saturday saw the murder, looting, and destruction continue on both the streets of London and some of the suburbs. This was a time to settle old scores. Masters were killed by resentful apprentices, and often debtors took advantage of the anarchy to kill those to whom they owed money. No one and nowhere were sacrosanct.

John Imworth, who had been the marshall at the now destroyed Marshalsea Prison in Southwark, had taken refuge in Westminster Abbey. We are told:

> ...A body of rioters entered the church, passed the altar rails, and tore the unhappy man away from the very shrine of Edward the Confessor, one of

Left: Portrait of Richard II, 'The Westminster Portrait', 1390s. This is the earliest known portrait of an English monarch, according to the abbey website.

Below: Edward the Confessor's mausoleum in the King's Chapel, Westminster Abbey, London, *c.* 1818. From here, Roger Legatt was dragged to his death in Cheapside. It was also here that Richard II prayed an hour later.

whose marble pillars he was embracing in the vain hope that the sanctity of the spot would protect him. He was dragged along to Cheapside, and there decapitated.[46]

On returning from Mile End, the King bypassed the tower, probably believing it to still be occupied by the rebels, whereas in fact they had long abandoned it. He returned instead to the Royal Wardrobe, Baynard's Castle, which was destroyed by the Great Fire in 1666, and was situated on the river front near Blackfriars Station. Richard's mother and the royal household would have been witnesses to the screaming of the victims, the parading of heads on poles, and the surrounding destruction. Action more decisive than simply giving into rebel demands was needed. Another meeting with the rebels was arranged, but this time in a venue about 0.5 miles to the north, at Smithfield.

Smithfield: The Final Chapter

The outline of Smithfield is well enough preserved to be able to construct and visualise the final dramatic chapter of the rebellion. At the time of the rebellion, the area of West Smithfield was mainly open field, but the Church of St Bartholomew and the hospital were situated where they are now.

Within an hour of John Imworth being dragged from the altar at Westminster Abbey, the King had gone to the abbey to take the sacrament at the very same altar that the unfortunate Imworth had been dragged from. He then rode to Smithfield to meet the insurgents. What happened next is best told by a chronicler who may well have been a witness to the events:

> Then the King caused a proclamation to be made that all the commons of the country who were still in London should come to Smithfield, to meet him there; and so they did. And when the King and his train had arrived there they turned into the eastern meadow in front of St Bartholomew's, which is a house of canons. And the commons arrayed themselves on the west side in great battles. Wat Tyler of Maidstone came to the King with great confidence, mounted on a little horse, that the commons might see him. And he dismounted, holding in his hand a dagger. And when he had dismounted he half bent his knee, and then took the King by the hand, and shook his arm forcibly and roughly, saying to him, 'Brother, be of good comfort and joyful, for you shall have, in the fortnight that is to come, praise from the commons even more than you have yet had, and we shall be good companions.' And the King said to Walter [Wat], 'Why will you not go back to your own country?' But the other answered, with a great oath, that neither he nor his fellows would depart until they had got their charter such as they wished to have it. And he

Eastern end of Smithfield with St Bartholomew's Church through the Tudor arch ahead. It was here in front of the hospital on the right that the King and his officials gathered, and where Tyler met his death. (*Author*)

To the left is the western end of Smithfield. It was here that Tyler and the rebels gathered, facing the King and his party at the eastern end on the right, in front of the hospital. (*Author*)

Mayor of London William Walworth and the demise of Wat Tyler in Smithfield (British Library Royal MS 18, *c.* 1385-1400). Depicting the end of the 1381 Peasant's Revolt, the image shows London's Mayor Walworth killing Wat Tyler.

demanded that there should be no more villeins in England, and no serfdom or villeinage, but that all men should be free and of one condition. To this the King gave an easy answer, and said that he should have all that he could fairly grant, reserving only for himself the regality of his crown. And then he bade him go back to his home, without making further delay.

Presently, Wat Tyler, in the presence of the King, sent for a flagon of water to rinse his mouth, because of the great heat that he was in, and when it was brought he rinsed his mouth in a very rude and disgusting fashion before the King's face. And then he made them bring him a jug of beer, and drank a great draught, and then in the presence of the King climbed on his horse again. At this time, a certain valet who was among the King's retinue, when he saw him, said aloud that he knew the said Walter for the greatest thief and robber in all Kent. And for these words Wat tried to strike him with his dagger, and would have slain him in the King's presence. But for his violent behaviour and despite, the Mayor of London William Walworth arrested him. And because he arrested him, the said Wat stabbed the mayor with his dagger in the stomach in great wrath.

But, as it pleased God, the Mayor was wearing armour and took no harm, but like a hardy and vigorous man drew his cutlass and struck back at the said Wat, and gave him a deep cut on the neck and then a great cut on the head. And during this scuffle, one of the King's household drew his sword and ran Wat two or three times through the body, mortally wounding him. Afterwards, the King sent out his messengers into divers parts to capture the malefactors and put them to death. And many were taken and hanged at London, and they set up many gallows around the City of London, and in other cities and boroughs of the south country. At last, as it pleased God, the King, seeing that too many of his liege subjects would be undone and too much blood spilt, took pity in his heart and granted them all pardon on condition that they should never rise again. And so finished this wicked war.[47]

We are told that after Tyler was struck down, he was 'rudely drawn by his hands and feet into the church of St Bartholomew, which was at hand.' (*Author*)

Another contemporary report, that of Henry Knighton, tells us that after Tyler was struck down, he was, 'Rudely drawn by his hands and feet into the church of St Bartholomew, which was at hand.'[48]

The church, one of the oldest remaining in London and founded AD 1123, remains a silent witness to these events. Froissart continues the final chapter for the rebellion in London:

> Thus these foolish people departed, some one way and some another; and the King and his lords and all his company right ordinately entered into London with great joy. And the first journey that the King made he went to the lady princess his mother, who was in a castle in the Royal called the Queen's Wardrobe, and there she had tarried two days and two nights right sore abashed, as she had good reason; and when she saw the King her son, she was greatly rejoiced and said, 'Ah, fair son, what pain and great sorrow that I have suffered for you this day!' Then the king answered and said, 'Certainly, madam, I know it well; but now rejoice yourself and thank God, for now it is time. I have this day recovered mine heritage and the realm of England, the which I had near lost.' Thus the king tarried that day with his mother, and every lord went peaceably to their own lodgings. Then there was a cry made in every street in the King's name, that all manner of men not being of the City of London and having not dwelt there the space of one year to depart; and if any such be found there the Sunday by the sun-rising, that they should be taken as traitors to the King and to lose their heads. This cry thus made, there was none that durst brake it, and so all manner of people departed and sparkled abroad every man to their own places. John Ball and Jack Straw were found in an old house hidden, thinking to have stolen away, but they could not, for they were accused by their own men. Of the taking of them the King and his lords were glad, and then strake off their heads and Wat Tyler's also, and they were set on London Bridge, and the valiant men's heads taken down that they had set on the Thursday before. These tidings anon spread abroad, so that the people of the strange countries, which were coming towards London, returned back again to their own houses and durst come no farther.[49]

Richard II's reign has been regarded as one of the worst in the history of England and has been blamed for creating the situation that would lead in the next century (1455-1485) to the dynastic struggle between the Houses of York and Lancaster, which became known as the Wars of the Roses.[50] In 1399, Richard was finally deposed by his Lancastrian cousin Henry Bolingbroke, who was crowned as Henry IV. He died in captivity around 14 February 1400, probably having been starved to death, and was brought for burial in the Church of All Saints, Kings Langley in Hertfordshire, on 6 March 1400.[51]

CHAPTER FOUR

The Jack Cade Rebellion, 1450

Background to the Uprising

The Cade Rebellion took place at a time in English history when the Lancastrian King Henry VI (1422-1461 and 1470-1471) had allowed the Crown to sink into debt. Henry was weak, easily led, extremely generous, and presided over a system that was corrupt. A contemporary and anonymous writer states:

> Then, and long before, England had been ruled by untrue counsel, wherefore the common profit was sore hurt and diseased, so that the common people, what with taxes and other oppressions, might not live by their handiwork and husbandry, wherefore they grudged sore against those who had the governance of the land.[52]

Henry was incapable of holding onto England's French possessions, much to the disgust of the mercantile classes. Governance was in decay. In this climate of high taxes, corruption, and the continuing loss of Normandy, the summer of 1450 saw a rebellion, which began in Kent under the leadership of an enigmatic leader Jack (or John) Cade. At the time, Henry VI suspected that Richard, Duke of York, was behind the uprising. It would only be five years before the commencement of the Wars of the Roses.

Cade also went by the names John Mortimer and John Amendalle. Cade's use of the name Mortimer, which was the family name of the Duke of York's mother, gave Henry concern that the Duke of York was somehow involved in the rebellion. This was denied by the rebels, but Cade's 'Complaint of the Commons of Kent', containing fifteen articles of accusation against the King's

Henry VI was mentally ill, suffering from bouts of insanity and periods of over-benevolence. His loss of England's French territories led to contempt among the mercantile classes, and the subsequent Cade Revolt.

officials in Kent, bore many similarities to the demands the Duke of York was to later make of Henry VI.[53] As has been said:

> The gentlemen of Kent saw a weak King, tossed between his upstart and wrangling nobles, and an alien [French] Queen with her thriftless hangers-on. The 'rebellion began shortly after the murder of the Duke of Suffolk. Suffolk had been the most unpopular of the King's inner circle and was widely regarded as a traitor. Henry, who relied on Suffolk, had little choice but to send him into exile, but Suffolk's ship, which was carrying him to France, was intercepted somewhere off Dover. The Duke, said to be the Queen's lover, was summarily tried on deck of his ship and executed with a rusty sword. Lord Say, Treasurer of England, and William Crowmer, Sheriff of Kent, both believed that it was Kentish men who were responsible for the murder and threatened to turn Kent into a deer forest as punishment. The rebels, in the late spring of 1450, issued a manifesto, 'The Complaint of The Poor Commons of Kent.'[54]

It would appear that he resembled Sir John Mortimer, a member of the opposition March family. Mortimer had been put to death accused of treason some years earlier. Now Cade, using the name, claimed to be his son.

Some Early Sources

There are a number of contemporary and early sources for the Cade Rebellion. Many of these are available in full on specialist websites and in print, recent editions:

MS Trinity College Dublin 509: *Bale's Chronicle*, and The Rebels' Petition. Three fifteenth century chronicles, edited by J. Gairdner (1880) deal with the rebellion in a political setting.

The Paston Letters, edited by J. Gairdner (1904) deal with accounts of the death of the Duke of Suffolk.
The Chronicle of the Grey Friars of London (Camden Society, 1852).
A Chronicle of London from 1089 to 1483.
The Great Chronicle of London, The New Chronicles of England and France.
Most of the Tudor chroniclers, Hall, Holinshed, and Stow deal with the rebellion, but it is likely that their sources are mainly the ones listed. Check dis

Some Key Places

The London Stone

London Stone now sits obscurely at pavement level on the north side of Cannon Street. It is probably an old Roman milestone, but its origins and purpose are obscure. It now has the appearance of a rounded boulder. It originally stood in the middle of Cannon Street and caused much damage to passing carriages. It was moved on a number of occasions in the eighteenth century.[55] It used to be set in the wall of St Swithins Church in Cannon Street. Its location now is about 50-yards west of St Swithins Lane. The historian William Camden (1551-1623), in his *Britannia*, writes, 'The stone called London Stone, from its situation in the centre of the longest diameter of the City, I take to have been a miliary, like that in the Forum at Rome, from whence all the distances were measured.'[56]
The London historian John Stow (*c.* 1525-1605) knew of the London Stone. He tells us:

> On the south side of this high street [Cannon Street], near unto the channel, is pitched upright a great stone, called London Stone, fixed in the ground very deep, fastened with bars of iron and otherwise so strongly set that if carts do run against it through negligence, the wheels be broken and the stone itself unshaken. The cause why this stone was set there, the time when, or other memory is none.[57]

A Survey of London comments that this is the:

> ...Very stone which the arch-rebel Jack Cade struck with his bloody sword when he had stormed London Bridge, and 'Now is Mortimer lord of this city' were the words he uttered too confidently as he gave the blow. Shakespeare, who perhaps wrote from tradition, makes him strike London Stone with his staff:

'Cade. Now is Mortimer lord of this city. And here, sitting upon London Stone, I charge and command that the conduit run nothing but claret wine this first year of our reign. And now henceforward it shall be treason for any that calls me Lord Mortimer.' Shakespeare, Second Part of Henry VI. Act IV. Scene vi.

The White Hart, Southwark

The White Hart is mentioned a number of times in early accounts of the rebellion as being the headquarters of Cade. It stood on the site of No. 61 (formerly 62) Borough High Street. It was burnt down in 1676 and finally demolished in 1889. The white hart was the badge of Richard II, which probably dates the original inn to the end of the fourteenth century.[58]

This hostelry is also mentioned in the context of the uprising by Shakespeare in Henry VI, part II. Cade thus addresses his followers: 'Will you needs be hanged with your pardons about your necks? Hath my sword therefore broke through London gates, that you should leave me at The White Hart in Southwark?'[59]

Fabyan, in his *Chronicles*, has the following entry: 'On 1 July 1450, Jack Cade arrived in Southwark, where he lodged at the "Hart", for he might not be suffered to enter the City.' The following deed of violence committed by Cade's followers

The London Stone in 2011, innocuously buried in the lower part of a building on the north side of Cannon Street, a short distance to the west of the junction with St Swithins Lane. (*Author*)

at this place is recorded in *The Chronicle of the Grey Friars*: 'At the Whyt Harte, in Southwarke, one Hawaydyne, of Sent Martyns, was beheddyd.'[60]

London and the Uprising

As with the Peasants' Revolt of 1381, there is a similarity in both the course of events and the places where the rebels created mayhem. The most noticeable difference here is that the revolt was lower gentry, middle, and merchant class based. On the basis that Cade passed himself off as the son of the Yorkist Earl of March, a dynastic opponent of the King, there was an element of Lancaster York opposition. Furthermore, the dislike of foreigners had not waned; one of the rebel demands read: 'You shall charge all Lumbards and strangers, being merchants, Genowais, Venetians, Florentines, and others this day to draw them together ... we shall have the heads of as many as we can get of them.'[61] As with the Peasants' Revolt nearly seventy years earlier, Cade's men assembled on Blackheath. By the first week of June 1450, approximately 20,000 men were assembled.

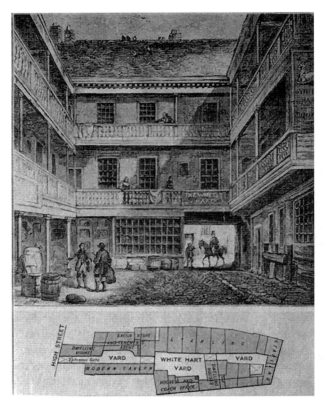

The White Hart Inn just prior to its demolition in 1889.

A contemporary source, *A Chronicle of London from 1089 to 1483*, reads:[62]

And in the moneth of June […] the comons of Kent assemblyd them in grete multytude, and chose to theym a capitayne, and named hym Mortymer, and cosyn to the duke of Yorke; but of note he was named Jak Cade. This kepte the people wonderously together, and made suche ordenaunces amonge theym, that he brought a great nombre of people of theym unto the Blak Heth, where he devysed a bylle of petycions to the kynge & his counsayll, and shewyd therin what iniuryes and oppressions the poore comons suffred by suche as were aboute the kynge, a fewe persones in nombre…[63]

Cade was encamped on Blackheath and the King was at the Priory of St John at Clerkenwell. The King sent a representative to Blackheath, who took back a copy of the rebel demands to the King, who showed them to his counsellors. These were at once rejected. The King's army of around 20,000 men was camped in Clerkenwell Fields. Cade, thinking that the King would launch an attack against him, and that he was outnumbered, withdrew to the friendlier surrounding of Sevenoaks, where he prepared for battle. The King foolishly divided his army into two, leaving half at Blackheath. The other half was sent to pursue Cade under Sir Humphrey Stafford and his brother William. We are told that Cade, who is referred to as the 'capitayne' here and throughout the document:

The road named after Jack Cade.

Drewe backe his people to a vyllage called Sevenok, and there enbataylled. Then it was agreed by the kynges counsayl, that sir Humfrey Stafforde, knyght, … with Wyllyam his brother, and other certayne gentylmen, shulde [give] chase, and the kynge with his lordes shulde retourne unto Grenewyche … But as before I have shewyd, when sir Humfrey with his company drewe nere unto Sevenok, he was warnyd of the capitayne [who] there abode with his people. And when he had counsayled with the other gentylmen, he, lyke a manfull knyght, sette vpon the rebellys and fought with theym longe; but in the ende, the capitayne slewe hym and his brother, with many other, & caused the rest to gyve backe [retreat].[64]

When news of the defeat reached the remainder of the King's army at Blackheath, the army mutinied; they ran riot through London, looting and burning. We are told:

Whan worde came of the overthrowe of the Staffordes, they sayd playnly boldly, that except [unless] the lorde Saye and other before reherced [mentioned] were comytted to warde [jail], they wolde take the capitaynes [Cade's] partye. For the appeasynge of whiche rumour, the lorde Saye was put into [the] Tower […] They began to murmur among themselves, some wishing the Duke of York home to aid the captain his cousin some.

As Helen Lyle, in her booklet *The Rebellion of Jack Cade: 1450*, says:

They demanded the heads of Lord Saye and Sele and five other others. To placate the soldiers and protect the victims the King put Saye and Crowmer in the Tower and sent to Cade, now again encamped at Blackheath, the Archbishop of Canterbury and the Duke of Buckingham to explore the ground and estimate the rebels' strength. They found him 'sober in talk, wise in reasoning, arrogant in heart, and stiff in opinion'. Their report was sufficiently unfavourable to spur the King's anxiety and he made plans to flee to Kenilworth, 'Beginning as much to doubt his own menial servants as his unknown subjects which spared not to speak that the Captain's cause was profitable to the Commonwealth.'[65]

There was much support for Cade in the city, and a meeting of 2 July voted to allow Cade entry. A fishmonger that opposed this move was jailed. The King and his court fled to the safety of Kenilworth Castle in the Midlands, and Cade advanced to Southwark. Cade, who still referred to himself as Mortimer, took up residence at the White Hart Inn, which was located in Borough High Street, Southwark. The inn, which became his headquarters, was convenient for London Bridge, and at that time, the sole means of entry to London.

On 2 July, the majority voted in favour of allowing Cade to enter London. At about 5 p.m. that afternoon, Cade and his followers left for London Bridge. The drawbridge was lowered, and as Cade:

Came upon the drawe brydge, he hewe [cut] the ropes that drewe the bridge, in senter with his sworde, and so passed into the cytie, and made in sondry places therof proclamacions in the kynges named that no man, [on] payne of dethe, shulde robbe or take any thynge [by] force without payinge therfore. By reason wherof he wonne many hertes of the comons of the cytie ; but all was done to begyle the people, as aftershall evydently appere. He rode thorough dyvers stretes of the cytie, and as he came by London stone, he strake it with his sworde, and sayd, 'Nowe is Mortymer lorde of this cytie.'

The occupants of the city were understandably concerned that discipline by Cade should be maintained. This was managed by Cade leading his men back out of the city into the fields at night, and punishing with death any rebels who transgressed. We are told, 'Cade did make strenuous efforts to keep his followers from "murder, rape, and robbery", even beheading at Blackheath a Captain Parys and his chief councillor, an ex-thief, Hawadyne...'[66]

Saturday 4 July saw the surrender to the rebels of Lord Saye and Crowmer. Lord Scales, the governor of the tower, in return for the handing over managed to retain control of the tower. This would ultimately save the situation. They were arraigned before the Lord Mayor at the Guildhall. The charges were general and the result a foregone conclusion: Saye asked at the Guildhall that he should, by right, be judged by his peers in the House of Lords, but 'the common people wished to have him killed at once in front of the justices'. Cade ordered the Lord Treasurer Lord Saye to be taken to the Standard in Cheapside, where he was beheaded forthwith without being allowed to finish his confession: 'The head was stuck on a spear and carried about the city by the rebels. The body was tied to a horse's tail and dragged across the bridge and through Southwark to St Thomas `a Waterings, where he was raised on a gallows and eventually quartered.'[67]

The Chronicle tells us that Sir James Cromer, the Sheriff of Kent and Saye's son-in-law, was [hurried] to 'Myles Ende, and there, in the capitaynes presence, byhedyd.'

The heads were placed on poles, and marched around the city. 'So savage had the Kentishmen become that they amused themselves by placing the heads together as though in the act of kissing.'[68] Following the execution of Sele's son-in-law Crowmer by the rebels at Mile End, Cade made the fatal mistake of alienating those in the city whose support he needed. The house of an ex-alderman, Malpas, and that of Cade's dinner host were looted. Cade himself took part in the robberies, thereby breaking his own code of conduct. Unity within the rebels suffered when that afternoon, one of Cade's inner circle was executed by the rebel faction. Cade had lost the hearts and minds of the people who feared the lapse in lawlessness would be directed at themselves. That evening, Cade and his followers returned to The White Hart in Southwark. On the other side of

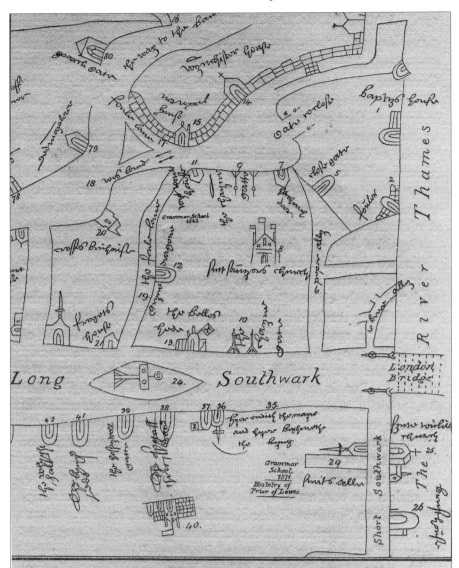

PART OF A PLAN OF SOUTHWARK, DATED 1540.
The original is in the Public Record Office.

On the right appears the Bridge-foot with the only representation of the stulpes or staple
which marked the limits of the Bridge. Lower down on the right is shown the Bridge
ouse (marked 26) in Short Southwark, now Tooley Street. *The White Hart* where Cade
t up appears in Long Southwark on the left (No. 42). The numbering is modern.

1. Baptys House.	24. The pillory.
2. Fouler.	10. The Chain Gates of St. Saviour's
3. Beere or Bear Alley.	Church.
25. St. Olave's Church.	8. St. Saviour's Church.
26. The Bridge House.	19. Foule Lane.
42. The White Hart Inn.	6. Pepper Alley.
41. The King's Head.	35. Here endeth the mayor and here
39. Gate of St. Thomas's Hospital.	beginneth the king.
38. The Hospital church door.	

the London Bridge, in the city, the mayor, the aldermen, and Lord Scales, who held the tower, met with a view to preventing Cade returning.

The Battle of London Bridge

On Sunday 5 July, the mayor and the aldermen approached the keeper of the tower Lord Scales and asked him for help in keeping Cade and the rebels from re-entering the city. Cade was in Southwark, and a number of men were given to Matthew Gough, a veteran captain, with a view to him blockading London Bridge. There are varying reports as to exactly what happened. Gordon Homes looks at the possibilities:

Honey Lane.

Above: The approach to Old London Bridge looking north from the Thames. (*Author*)

Left: The approach to Old London Bridge looking north from the Thames. (*Author*)

Gough may have been attacked before his plans for holding the Bridge had been put into execution, for we do not hear of any attempt to replace the severed ropes of the drawbridge nor of the closing of the gates and the lowering of the portcullises [...] in some way knowledge that the Bridge was being occupied by the mayor and citizens in strong force reached the rebels...[69]

London Bridge itself was not an ideal battleground, being covered in shops and houses. The central thoroughfare was only 8-foot wide. There are a number of early accounts that describe, with some differing minor detail, what happened next. Scales handed command of his men to veteran captain Matthew Gough, who sometime between 10 p.m. and midnight:

Set upon the rebels [...] killing the watch and ward on the bridge [...] A most fierce struggle began almost instantly. For the first time in its history, the whole length of the old structure was to be the scene of a desperate fight. All night long the conflict continued, and the rebels [...] were prepared to die fighting [...] The Kentishmen regained the southern end as far as the drawbridge, and being desperate, they deliberately set fire to the houses on either side, seemingly indifferent to the fate of the unfortunate inhabitants who had stayed in their houses since Cade's first coming.[70]

At one stage we are told that as hour after hour the fighting continued, the Londoners were pushed back as far as the Church of St Magnus, before finally turning the tables on the Kentishmen and pushing them back as far as Southwark.[71]

The contemporary sources give slightly varying accounts, but as Home in his *Old London Bridge* observes, 'For the first time in its history, the whole length of the old structure was to be the scene of a desperate fight.'[72]

All night long the conflict continued, and the rebels, doubtless realising that the success or failure of the rising hinged on their access to the City, were prepared to die fighting. Gough's first orders were to hold the Southwark Bridge-foot and not to advance at all until daylight, but gradually, in spite of the greatest efforts, the Londoners were driven back from the posts at the Bridge-foot until the Kentishmen had regained the southern end as far as the drawbridge, and being desperate, they deliberately set fire to the houses on either side, seemingly indifferent to the fate of the unfortunate inhabitants, who had stayed in their houses since Cade's first coming into the City.

Hall, in his history of London, collated between 1548 and 1550, captures the feeling of the awful events that night on London Bridge:

The car park and what remains of the churchyard for the Church of St Magnus, looking towards the Thames, which was the original entrance way to Old London Bridge where fighting took place. (*Author*)

Alas! What sorow it was to beholde that miserable chaunce; for some desyringe to eschew the fyre lept on hys enemies weapon, and so died; fearfull women, with chyldren in their armes, amased and appalled, lept into the river; others, doubtinge how to save them self betwene fyre, water, and swourd, were in their houses suffocated and smoldered; yet the captayns nothyng regarding these chaunces, fought on this drawe-bridge all the nyghte valeauntly, but in conclusion, the rebelles got the drawe-bridge and drowned many, and slew John Sutton, alderman, and Robert Heysande, a hardy citizen, with many other, besyde Matthew Gough, a man of greate wit, much experience in feates of chivalrie, the which in continuall warres had valeantly served the king, and his father, in the partes beyond the sea. But it is often sene, that he which many tymes hath vanquyshed his enemies in straunge countreys, and returned agayn as a conqueror, hath of his owne nation afterward been shamfully murdered and brought to confusion. This hard and sore conflict endured on the bridge till nine of the clocke in the mornynge in doubtfull chaunce and fortune's balaunce: for some tyme the Londoners were bet back to the stulpes [bridge base] at Saint Magnus Corner; and sodaynly agayne the rebelles were repulsed and dryven back to the stulpes in Southwarke; so that both partes beyng faynte, wery, and fatygate [fatigued], agreed to desist from fight, and to leve battayll till the next day, vpon condition that neyther Londoners should passe into Southwarke, nor the Kentish men into London.[73]

The Demise of Cade

Cade and his associates had looked to return to Kent with their booty, but for Cade it was not to be. *A New History of London* tells us:

> Perceiving that his affairs were now become desperate, Cade thought it advisable to provide for his own safety, together with that of his rich booty, which he sent by water to Rochester; and he himself in disguise fled into the woody part of Sussex. A proclamation was issued by the government, offering 1,000 marks to any person that should bring him, either dead or alive. He was discovered lurking in a garden at Hothfield in Sussex, by Alexander Eden, a Kentish gentleman, who killed him, and having put his body into a cart, brought it to London, where he received the promised reward.[74]

In order to confirm the corpse really was Jack Cade, the cart stopped at his former headquarters, the White Hart Inn in Southwark, where the landlady identified the body. We are then told that from here the body was taken to the nearby King's Bench Prison where the remains were kept from the Monday to the following Thursday evening.[75]

> His head with those of nine of his associates were placed on London Bridge; and some other of the ringleaders were tried and executed. Quiet was thus restored; but the dispersed populace carried home with them sentiments, which fomenting the public discontent, disposed the people to listen to the Duke of York's pretensions, which now became a general topic of discussion.[76]

CHAPTER FIVE

The First and Second Battles of St Albans: 1455 and 1461

Background: Wars of the Roses

This was a complex series of wars, or more accurately, battle-sized family feuds, which lasted thirty-two years from the First Battle of St Albans in 1455 to the final battle at Stoke Field in 1487. The wars are complex because of the number of noble families involved that took part were slain and replaced by children and assorted relatives, all looking for revenge. Participants changing sides and the ongoing involvement of the Earl of Warwick (Warwick the Kingmaker), who also had a tendency to change sides, makes this a confusing series of battles to follow. The wars were a result of a power struggle around Henry VI (1421-1471), who was the great-grandson of John of Gaunt, and Henry's cousin, Richard Duke of York. Edward finally defeated Henry in 1471 at the Battle of Tewkesbury. The Wars of the Roses finally came to an end with the establishment of the Tudor dynasty under Henry VII.[77]

Henry was deeply pious, unwarlike, weak-willed, and simple-minded. He was unequal to the business of controlling the corruption of the nobles that surrounded him. He also had a habit of slipping in and out of coma-like periods where government was all but impossible. In 1447, he started a feud by promoting the Duke of Somerset over Richard Duke of York, which would come to a head at St Albans in 1455. In 1453, Henry managed to lose more French territories, and became mentally ill; he was now ineffective. But despite this, in 1453 his wife Margaret gave birth to a son, Edward of Lancaster, Prince of Wales. She now saw the Duke of York as a threat to her new-born son's inheritance. This became apparent in March 1454 when Parliament made the Duke of York Protector and Defender of the Realm. When Henry recovered from his illness, he remembered nothing of previous events. York had no choice but to resign; his supporters believed that Margaret and Somerset would see them as a future threat and crush them. By 1455, the Duke of York and his supporters decided it would be safer to strike first. In May 1455, the Yorkists, including the Earl of Warwick and the Earl of Salisbury, while proclaiming loyalty to Henry, marched south towards London with the aim of 'removing' the Duke of Somerset. It is likely that contemporary claims that York had between 5,000 and 7,000 men were exaggerated; 3,000 men is more likely.[78]

Early Sources

There are a large number of contemporary and early descriptions of both battles, some available on-line at http://www.british-history.ac.uk. One of the most immediate is the 'Calendar of State Papers and Manuscripts in the Archives and Collections of Milan: 1385-1618'. The following is an example of its style and ability to draw the reader into a world long past:

> …My lord of Somerset ruled as usual. Subsequently, I learned here yesterday […] that fresh disturbances broke out in England a few days after my departure. A great part of the nobles have been in conflict, and the Duke of Somerset, the Earl of Northumberland, and my lord of Clifford are slain, with many other lords and knights on both sides. The Duke of Somerset's son … was mortally wounded; my lord of Buckingham and his son are hurt. The Duke of York has done this with his followers. On the 24th, he entered London and made a solemn procession to St Pauls. They say he has demanded pardon from the king for himself and his men, and will have it. He will take up the government again, and some think that the affairs of that kingdom will now take a turn for the better. If that be the case, we can put up with this inconvenience…[79]

Another source frequently referred to is eye-witness to the skirmish, the Abbot of St Albans, John of Wheathampstead, who left a graphic account of what he saw and played host to Henry VI at the abbey. His account has to date not been translated from the Latin. Another is Gregory's Chronicle, otherwise referred to as the *Chronicle of London* by William Gregory, a London skinner and mayor of the fifteenth century. The English is Chaucerian in style, but descriptive and interesting to follow.

The First Battle of St Albans: 22 May 1455

By 7 a.m., York, Salisbury, and Warwick, with divers knights and squires, arrived at Keyfield. A couple of hours later, the royal party marched into St Peter's Street.

As was customary, an exchange of messages took place between the two parties. York demanded that Henry hand over the Duke of Somerset, 'The man disloyal to his country who ruined Normandy, whose negligence lost Gascony, and who reduced the entire realm of England to a state of misery.' With Somerset undoubtedly standing next to the King and reading the message, the reply was perhaps inevitable: 'Void the field [or] I shall destroy […] every mother's son and they [shall] be hanged, drawn, and quartered that may be taken afterward.'[80] The Yorkists prepared for battle, while the Lancastrians, despite the tone of the negotiations, thought that the quarrel would be sorted by negotiation. Thus, when the attack came the Lancastrians were far from prepared. Many were sitting around, and many had yet to put on their armour.

The Battle Location

St Albans was an open town with no walls for protection. The Duke of York had set up camp on the east side of St Albans, which is now the Keyfield Car Park.

As Peter Burley observes:

> Keyfield must be one of England's least celebrated historical sites. Nothing here commemorates the fact that it was on this very spot that the Wars of the Roses started. In the assembly ground in front of the ditch – now a car park –

Keyfield carpark, viewed from the beer garden near Tonman Ditch, where the Duke of York and his army set up camp. This is where the War of the Roses began. (*Author*)

soldiers buckled their armour and strung their bows before that very first order was given in the wars to advance and engage the king's forces in combat.[81]

The royal army made the Moot Hall their head-quarters. Although St Albans was not a walled town, there was a ditch around the town, called the Tonman Ditch. Behind the ditch there was a rampart surmounted variously by some sort of hedge, fence, or palisade along its length. The buildings backing onto the ditch were known as the 'town backsides'. Three roads crossed the ditch and entered St Albans from the east: these were Cock Lane (now called Hatfield Road), Shropshire Lane (now called Victoria Street), and Sopwell Lane [...] Thick wooden beams or 'Bars' could be quickly dragged across to block these roads. As soon as the Lancastrians had occupied the centre of the town, orders were given to man the Bars and the fence in case of a Yorkist attack. Lord Clifford, an experienced soldier, was put in charge of these defences. He was assisted by commanders such as Sir Bertine Entwistle and Sir Richard Harrington, both veterans of the French Wars...

The Lancastrians, under King Henry VI, occupied the town itself. Henry stayed at a house near Market Place. Peter Burley states, 'The Royal Standard was raised in St Peter's [...] It must have been close to the old Town Hall, probably near the present-day Boots store!'[82]

The nineteenth century *Guide to Hertfordshire* observes what happened next:

A most sanguinary battle ensued, in which the king was totally defeated, and about 800 of his partisans were slain, including the Duke of Somerset, the Earls of Stafford and Northumberland [...] and many others of rank and distinction. The King himself was taken prisoner by the Duke of York in a small cottage, where he had taken shelter, entirely deserted by his friends, and wounded in the neck by an arrow. He was conveyed to the Abbey, and kindly entertained by the Abbot.[83]

Four of the King's bodyguard were killed and the Royal Standard was abandoned.

At 10 a.m., the Yorkists attacked in the area of Sopwell and Shropshire Lane Bars. For half an hour there was stalemate, following which Warwick and Ogle lead an attack on the market place, approaching through the gardens and back of the town. Warwick attacked through the back gardens through Holywell Hill and into St Peter's Street between The Keys and The Chequers inns.

Fighting in Market Place and the town square was fierce. At the northern end of the town, York's troops entered St Peter's Street, killing all that stood in their way. Abbot John of Wheathampstead described the scene: 'Here you saw one fall with his brains dashed out, there another with a broken arm, a third with a cut throat, and a fourth with a pierced chest, and the whole street was full of

Here, in front of The White Hart tap, the Wars of the Roses began in what is now the Keyfield carpark. The Tonman Ditch runs through The White Hart beer garden. Looking down is to look at where the Wars of the Roses began. (*Author*)

Here in Sopwell Lane, the Earl of Salisbury attacked the Bar held by Lord Clifford's men. (*Author*)

Henry VI raised the Royal Standard in the vicinity of what is now the Boots store in St Peters Street. It was here that he was injured in the neck by an arrow. The market place lies a short distance to the left. (*Author*)

The market place ran with blood. Abbot Wheathampstead, watching close-by from the abbey gatehouse, stated, 'Here you saw one fall with his brains dashed out, there another with a broken arm, a third with a cut throat, and a fourth with a pierced chest, and the whole street was full of dead corpses'. (*Author*)

Incorrectly placed plaque on the wall of the Skipton building society. Somerset was slain opposite. (*Author*)

Here on the corner of Victoria Street and Market Place, the Duke of Somerset died fighting, killing four opponents before being cut down by a poleaxe. The plaque is opposite, on Skipton building society. In the background to the right is the site of the old Moot Hall. (*Author*)

dead corpses.' Somerset took shelter in The Castle Inn just off Market Place. He was soon surrounded and died fighting. A primary source, the Dijon Relation, describes the demise of Somerset:[84]

> York's men at once began to fight Somerset and his men, who were within the house and defended themselves valiantly. In the end, after the doors were broken down Somerset saw he had no option but to come out with his men, as a result of which they were all surrounded by the Duke of York's men. After some were stricken down and the Duke of Somerset had killed four men by his own hand, so it is said, he was felled to the ground with an axe, and at once wounded in so many places that he died.

By 11 a.m., the fighting was over. Wheathampstead tells us that on scenting victory, they started to run through the streets and loot: '…Especially the Northerners, broke into the houses, stealing gold and silver plate, money and wine […] those of the King's party who survived had been robbed, "Despoiled of horse and harness."'[85] During the course of the afternoon, the town was looted, prisoners rounded up, and the dead removed.[86]

The Aftermath

It left maybe 800 persons dead including the Duke of Somerset, the Earl of Northumberland, and Lord Clifford on the King's side, and Lord Clinton and Sir Robert Ogle amongst the Yorkists.[87] As mentioned, the King had been injured in the neck by an arrow and was 'taking refuge' in a nearby tradesman's house. The wounded King was escorted for safety to the abbey, where he remained overnight. Other members of the royal party to take refuge there was the injured Duke of Buckingham, who had been struck in the face by an arrow, and the lord treasurer and standard bearer, the exceptionally vain Earl of Wiltshire. Wiltshire had dumped his armour and taken up the disguise of a monk's habit. Gregory says he 'fought mainly with the heels, for he was frightened of losing his beauty'.[88]

The Abbey

After the Yorkist success:

> York, Salisbury, and Warwick entered what is now the Cathedral and approached the king, who was effectively their captive. It is likely that the events described took place in the area, which is now open to the air. On

St Alban's Abbey. The open area to the left is the site of the original church where Henry VI, having been wounded by an arrow in the neck, was taken after the first battle. (*Author*)

The Lady Chapel, St Alban's Abbey. Under the floor many of the principle nobles, Somerset, Clifford, and Northumberland were buried after the First Battle. (*Author*)

bended knees they begged his forgiveness for having put his life in peril. They assured the king that they were loyal subjects who never meant to harm him, only the traitors around him such as Somerset [...] Henry forgave them he obviously had little choice in the matter..

CHAPTER SIX

The Second Battle of St Albans: Shrove Tuesday, 17 February 1461

The Prelude

In December 1460, at Sandal Castle, Wakefield, the Lancastrians took revenge on the Yorkists, killing over 2,000 including the Duke of York. The severed heads of York, Rutland, (York's second son), and Salisbury were placed on spikes at York over Micklegate Bar, the western gate through the York city walls. York's head bore a paper crown and a sign saying, 'Let York overlook the town of York.' *The Gregory Chronicle* tells us that after Wakefield, the Lancastrians, under Queen Margaret and Edward Prince of Wales, headed south, looting, raping, and causing destruction as they went.[89] The politics now changed: the Yorkist cause was now lead by nineteen-year-old Edward, Earl of March and heir to the throne, and the Earl of Warwick.

On the morning of 12 February, Warwick left London, marching to St Albans. Edward was tied up facing the Lancastrians at Mortimer Cross, where he was successful, but left Warwick to face the 'northern hordes' alone. As Burley comments, 'In 1455, the Lancastrians had been defending St Albans; in 1461, it was the Yorkists who were trying to hold the town. Warwick's decision to place his army at St Albans meant that for a second time in less than six years the town would become a bloody battlefield.'[90]

The Background

Warwick was holding King Henry as a captive. Queen Margaret and her army, which included French, Scottish, and Welsh mercenaries, were heading for London, and Warwick needed to block her. The march south had been marred by widespread looting, rape, and plunder, causing panic in anticipation. Warwick arrived three days early and chose a position north of St Albans covering the Sandridge and Harpenden roads, which are the modern A1081 and B651 respectively. His left wing was under the command of his brother John Neville, Lord Montagu, who was deployed near the modern day 'Ancient Briton' junction. It is possible that the right wing was commanded as far as Nomansland Common by the Duke of Norfolk. Archers were placed in the town itself.[91] At the main road from the north he set up several fixed defences, including cannons and obstacles such as caltrops and pavises studded with spikes, partly manned by Burgundian mercenaries equipped with handguns. Part of his defences used the ancient Belgic earthwork known as Beech Bottom Dyke, which still survives in an impressive and walkable stretch. Due to the treachery of one of Warwick's stewards, Margaret knew of Warwick's defences, which were based on an attack from the north. Margaret's forces moved towards St Albans at night and attacked from the direction of the abbey, coming from the direction of Roman Verulamium. Warwick's Yorkist army probably ranged at somewhere between 8,000 and 12,000 men, and Margaret's Lancastrian army in the region of 15,000 men. The Lancastrian force was headed by Henry Beaufort, Third Duke of Somerset, who has been described as a 'Ruthless and violent man obsessed with vengeance, but flawed by fecklessness and faithlessness...'

The Battle

At dawn on 17 February, the Queen's army attacked the Yorkists already occupying the town. They crossed the River Ver, in the vicinity of St Michael's church, advanced up Fishpool Street, Romeland Hill, and George Street until they reached the market place. They were fired on by Yorkist archers in the town centre who shot at them from the windows of the surrounding buildings. The Lancastrians were pushed back down George Street and regrouped at the River Ver ford. A second attack, which met with no opposition, was launched around the edge of the town before crossing the town ditch and advancing up what is now Folly Lane and Catherine Street. They were now able to attack the archers from the rear.

The situation was now confused with Lancastrians fighting at the western and northern end of town, with the Yorkist archers in between and also further out at Bernards Heath and Sandridge. House to house fighting continued for a number of hours, until the Yorkists' force of archers in the town were destroyed. The Lancastrians rested for a short while, and then pushed out of the town past St Peter's Church and on to Bernards Heath.

The Lancastrian army crossed the River Ver here at this bridge, which was substantially rebuilt in 1765.

English Weather

Montagu now attempted to turn his force to the south-west to confront the Lancastrians while looking in vain for reinforcements from Warwick. The positions originally taken up by Warwick made it very difficult for him to reverse, and combined with treachery and a defection by Sir Henry Lovelace, Warwick was struggling to hold the town. Things now went from bad to worse. The Yorkists were relying on their Burgundian gunners, but it is likely that because of the damp and snow the powder for the Yorkist handguns and cannons became damp and made the weapons unusable. Eighteen of the Burgundians managed to either blow themselves up or set themselves on fire.[92] 'With their guns useless and many of their archers killed or captured in St Albans, Montagu's men had little choice but to engage the advancing Lancastrians in fierce hand-to-hand fighting. The fighting on Bernards Heath became a grim slugging match, with both sides anxiously waiting for reinforcements.'[93]

As the day had progressed, the Lancastrian ranks became increasingly swelled by an inflow of men from Dunstable. No reinforcements came for the Yorkists. They became demoralised by their own fleeing soldiers:

> Montagu's men were steadily pushed back across Bernards Heath until eventually the pressure became too much and the Yorkists broke and fled [...] One account talks of the fleeing Yorkists being caught up in thickets. The main

Bernards Heath: The fighting on Bernards Heath became a grim slugging match, with both sides anxiously waiting for reinforcements. It was here that the Yorkist forces broke and fled. The site of the gallows and old burial ground are immediately to the left.

Nomansland Common, where the Yorkists rallied for a last stand and the exhausted Lancastrians withdrew to St Albans. Warwick probably retreated down Ferrers Road, to the right of the car park.

road across the heath was used for cattle droving, suggesting a wide clear route, so the soldiers may have become disordered on this grassland and may have fled into the surrounding scrub.[94]

Montagu was captured. The Yorkist line of retreat to London was blocked. Warwick reached Bernard's Heath, but it was now too late. Warwick made a fighting retreat through Sandridge and Nomansland Common and managed to slip away during the night with 4,000 men.

As the Yorkist lines had collapsed, they lost control of the King. Henry's tent had been pitched under an oak tree on Bernards Heath. According to some reports, Henry spent the battle laughing and singing, although it is not recorded whether this was because he was delighted to see the Yorkists being defeated. There are various versions of how Henry defected to the Lancastrians.

Aftermath: Put Not Your Trust in Princes

Henry VI was now reunited with his wife Margaret, and son, and stayed in the abbey as guests of Abbot Whethamstede.

After the withdrawal of the Yorkists, the King needed protection. Two Yorkist knights, the sixty-eight-year-old Lord William Bonville, constable of Exeter Castle (1393-1461), and Sir Thomas Kyriell behaved honourably and had sworn to Henry that they would not let him come to any harm; they remained with him throughout, even though they could easily have retreated with the departing Yorkist forces. Henry had promised them both immunity – a hollow promise. Bonville, Kyriell, and other prisoners were brought before Henry, Margaret, and the seven-year-old Edward. It is reported that Margaret, overriding Henry, turned to her son and asked, 'Fair son, what death shall these two knights die?' The child replied, 'Let them have their heads taken off.' A stunned Bonville, who had believed Henry's word, told the child, 'May God destroy those who taught thee this manner of speech.' Despite Henry's pleas of mercy for the two knights, the executions were carried out the next day, 18 February.[95] John Neville, who had also been captured and might have shared the same fate, was lucky; the Duke of Somerset feared that his own younger brother, who was in Yorkist hands, might be executed in reprisal and thus spared Neville.

Despite Margaret's victory and open path to London, the northern Lancastrian army's reputation for pillage caused the Londoners to bar the gates. She and her hordes returned north with their plunder. Edward and Warwick entered London on 2 March, and Edward was proclaimed King Edward IV of England. A few weeks later, on 29 March 1461, he confirmed his position with a decisive victory at the Battle of Towton, near York. This was the largest and bloodiest battle ever to take place on British soil.

Left: Detail from a larger illustration of the ruthless, ambitious Margaret of Anjou, wife of King Henry VI. The original source is a manuscript illuminated by the Talbot Master in Rouen *c.* 1430-60. (*British Library*)

Below: Built 1403-1412, the bell, which dates from 1335 and is named Gabriel, was rung during the First Battle of St Albans as a call to arms for the Lancastrian troops in the town centre. The site of the Eleanor Cross is in front of the tower in Market Place, where the archers drove back the Lancastrians.

Burial of the Dead

By the time of the battles, there was an arrangement that ordinary burials would take place in St Peter's graveyard.[96]

The *Entwistle Family History*[97] tells us:

The brass remained entire until the eighteenth century when, during repairs to the Church, the stone on which it was laid was broken to pieces by the workmen and the upper part lost. The remaining half, after much enquiry, was discovered in 1797. There is a drawing of the monument in the

Northern end of St Peter's Churchyard. The likely burial place of many of the fallen. An early source states: 'This church and churchyard was stuffed full with the bodies of such as were slain in the two battles, fought here at St Albans'. (*Author*)

Chancel of St Peter's. Under the floor lie three Lancastrians killed in the first battle: Sir Bertine Entwistle, who was wounded in the shoulder and died a few days later. Ralf and Ralf Babthorpe (father and son), who were part of Northumberland's retinue. Another Lancastrian, Thomas Packington of Hampton Lovett, Worcestershire. The memorial is lost, but they probably lie in the same crypt. (*Author*)

The brass of Sir Bertine Entwistle, killed by a severe sword wound to the shoulder in the First Battle and buried under the floor of St Peter's. The brass was damaged by builders in 1797. The remaining lower half is in the British Museum. (*Tom Entwistle*)

British Museum […] so far back as 1611 […] The whole was in a perfect state.

St Peter's Church at the northern end of the town would have been the natural place for the burial of the common war dead. It was in the immediate vicinity of fierce fighting and there are a series of stories associated with burials here. Weever, writing at the beginning of the seventeenth century, tells us:

> This church and churchyard was stuffed full with the bodies of such as were slain in the two battles, fought here at St Albans; in which I find a funeral monument for my valiant countryman Sir Bertine Entwissel, who fighting on the King's party, died of a wound received in the first battle...

He continues: 'Ralph Babthorpe, the father, and Ralph, the son of Babthorpe, in the east riding of Yorkshire […] fighting in this town under the banner of K[ing] Henry VI, lost their lives, and here lie buried together.'[98]

The *Entwistle Family History*, referring to an early history, tells us that that Sir Bertine Entwistle was buried 'under the place of the Lecterne in the Quier, where there is a memorial of him'.[99]

Another immediate connection to the battle comes through Weever's observation of a tomb within the church, but no longer present of Edmund Westby, a justice of the peace. Weever says that Henry VI, 'Was in thus Edmund's house during the time of the first battle in the town.'[100]

In 1893, the church sexton told a local historian that 'he was always turning up bits and pieces on the north side of the graveyard that he attributed to the burials after the battles'.[101] Another oft repeated story is that of a mass grave in the churchyard, with an account of the 'bodies being buried in a trench, standing,

Beech Bottom approaching railway crossing where human bones, probably relating to the battle, were found during the building of the railway. (*Author*)

Bernards Heath: The gallows and an old, now-lost burial ground were sited where the flats are located. This would have been a logical burial spot. (*Author*)

still in full armour, and being frozen solid because of the weather [in February 1461].'[102] Another likely place of burial is the site of the an old, lost burial ground on Bernards Heath, which stood close to the gallows. The site now lies under a block of flats.

As a rule, the nobility found more illustrious resting places. The burial place of Edmund Beaufort, Duke of Somerset, killed in the First Battle –he, Lord Clifford, and Henry Percy, Earl of Northumberland, was the Lady Chapel of St Alban's Abbey, now the cathedral. In Gough's *Sepulchral Monuments* (Vol. Ii, part ii, p.177), it is stated that during the latter part of the eighteenth century, the floor was dug into for repairs and, 'Some large bones were found, which were adjudged to be Henry Percy, Earl of Northumberland. He was one of the three nobles interred [t]here in 1455.'[103]

CHAPTER SEVEN

The Battle of Barnet, 14 April 1471: Wars of the Roses

Background

The Battle of Barnet, which took place on the foggy Easter morning of 14 April 1471, is probably one of the most important battles of the Wars of the Roses. It started at around 5 a.m. in the morning and lasted between 3 and 4 hours. As will be seen, there is little that is certain with regards to anything to do with the battle, such as the numbers involved, numbers killed, or the positioning of the opposing armies themselves. However, it is generally accepted that the Yorkist army numbered in the region of 10,000 men and the Lancastrians 15,000. The Yorkist contingent was led by King Edward VI and the Lancastrians by the Earl of Warwick. Aside from the large number of nobility slain, the battle saw the death of Warwick 'the Kingmaker' and the re-establishment of Edward IV on the throne. It has been observed that somewhere on that foggy Easter Monday, the day of the battle, three Kings of England were present on the field at Barnet: Henry VI, Edward IV, and Richard III. Estimates of losses vary wildly, but probably range somewhere between 1,500 and 4,000 souls. Many would have suffered horrific wounds.

Uncertain Location

For such a significant battle, there is very little that allows us to pinpoint the exact location or orientation of the battle. There is an obelisk that was erected in 1740 at Hadley Highstone alongside the Great North Road to mark the spot where Warwick was killed, but even that has been moved from its original

The obelisk at the junction of Dury Road and the Great North Road, erected by
Jeremy Sambrook in 1740 at Monken Hadley, on the site of the Battle of Barnet.
A cannon ball was supposedly found nearby around 170 years ago. (*Author*)

position. At the time of writing, there is a move in place by the Battlefield Trust to undertake detailed surveys, archaeological digs, and attempt to determine the boundaries, as was recently achieved with the relocating of the site of the Battle of Bosworth in Leicestershire. This lack of certainty, curiously enough, has done little to reduce the experience of walking the likely area of the battlefield. We have enough contemporary or nearly contemporary sources to be able to put a broad brush on the location where the fighting took place, but at this time no provable archaeological evidence; purely, we have reliance on a number of contemporary sources, none of which provide enough conclusive geographical evidence. Physical evidence such as exists is tenuous. Richard Brooke, a battlefield enthusiast, walked the area of the battle in July 1856. He comments: 'W. Hutton, F.S.A, states that the keeper of the Red Cow tavern, near the obelisk [...] preserve a ball of a pound and a half weight, which he dug out of the ground.'[104]

In a footnote, Brooke observes that 'a respectable person' who had lived in the area for fifty-six years, on being asked about battlefield relics, stated that 'he did not know of his own knowledge that any relics of the battle had been discovered; but that he had heard of such discoveries formerly.'[105] There are cannon balls, but no proof that they originated from the battle itself. The only means we have at the moment of locating the site of the battle are a number of early written sources, dating back to within days of the battle.

The Primary Sources

For a comprehensive list and interesting analyses of the sources for the Battle of Barnet there is a short booklet called the *Chroniclers of the Battle of Barnet*, and a chapter of *Barnet: 1471*, which analyses the strengths and shortcomings of the various sources, which number about a dozen.[106] More recently, an extensive study of the possible location of the battle has been undertaken by a local resident, Brian Warren, who has produced an interesting and well-argued booklet, which argues that the accepted location of the battle site, stretching across Hadley Green with opponents facing north-south, is incorrect. He argues that the battle took place a small distance to the north on a north-south battle line. There is also an argument that the battle may have taken place on an east-west axis across the Great North Road.

Either way, Warren argues that Warwick was located on higher ground in the present Wrotham Park, and that the King was down the slope in Enfield Chase; this would explain guns being fired by Warwick all night and hitting nobody, for the shot was angled over the heads of the Yorkists.[107]

One source, which lay undiscovered until around fifty years ago, is a letter home written by Gerhard von Wesel, a Hanseatic merchant who was living in London at the time of the battle. It was written three days after the battle and says:

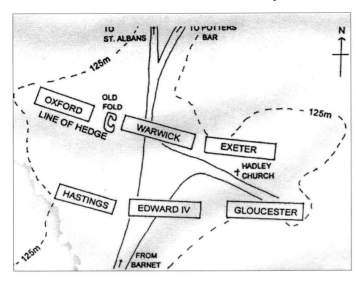

This is the accepted, but now heavily challenged view of the battle. (*Brian Warren*)

Warwick and his liegemen and followers, who had been at Coventry, pitched camp a mile beyond the said village [Barnet], right beside the St Albans high road, on a broad green. King Edward's followers, not knowing exactly in the darkness where their opponents were, rode on to that same place in the night and pitched their camp on the other side of the aforementioned high road in a hollow, on marshy ground, right opposite Warwick.

A letter from a Lancastrian combatant Sir John Paston, written four days after the battle in which he and his brother fought, refers to the battle being fought 0.5 miles from Barnet.

The implication of von Wesel's description is that Warwick camped on Hadley Green. Other sources imply that Warwick camped along the north-south axis of the Great North Road in the vicinity of a line of hedges. Probably the most used source for describing the battle, which was particularly referred to in nineteenth century accounts, is the anonymous *Historie of the Arrivall of Edward IV*. It was written by the end of May 1471 by somebody who describes himself as a servant of Edward IV. Edward adopted the work as his official war history.[108]

Theories have been put forward on the location and dynamics of the battle. In brief, there is dispute as to whether the axis of the battle was aligned north-south, east-west, or something in between. Conjecture is based on the number of soldiers involved and the space they would have needed to occupy, the nature of the territory, and the wording of the primary accounts. If St Mary's Church (Hadley Church), the manor, and certain windmills covered the area of the battlefield, why did none of the sources mention them as being relevant to the battle?

There are two works as of 2011 that deal analytically with the questions posed by the lack of physical evidence of the battlefield itself, the positioning of the armies, and where the large number of dead (numbering well into the thousands) are buried. These are an 1882 treatise by local clergyman Frederick Cass and two works by local historian Brian Warren. Both are based on interpretation of the key primary sources,[109] local knowledge as to the landscape, and how army commanders would have been likely to use the landscape to their advantage, bearing in mind that the Easter morning on which the 4 hour battle took place was obscured in fog.

Warwick, marching from the north, had over a day to choose his position, which was somewhere between a 0.5 and 1 mile north of Barnet on what is now the Great North Road, or A1000. When Edward arrived the evening before, he approached from London through the town of Barnet. It was already dark, and a thick fog had set in. He was within yards of the Lancastrians, but neither side could see the other, so the ability to conventionally line up against each other face to face was lost. It is this that has led to difficulty in pinpointing the opposing army positions. Cass summarises: 'A haze of uncertainty hangs over the details of the engagement, though the accounts of several of the old chroniclers were compiled within comparatively few years afterwards.' He notes that the numbers of participants and those slain vary dramatically in each of the accounts. Cass quotes some earlier sources that confirm uncertainty as to the precise site of the battle:

> Salmon, in his *History of Hertfordshire*, says that 'the place which the present inhabitants take for the Field of Battle is a green spot near Kick's-Und, [Kitts End] between the St Alban's Road and the Hatfield Road, a little before they meet'. It is near this that Sir Jeremy Sambrooke's obelisk now stands, and here it was, according to tradition, that Warwick fell [...] Far more likely is it [...] both from this consideration and from the configuration of the ground, that the line occupied by Warwick's army was drawn nearer to Barnet, extending in the direction of Hadley Church eastwards and crossing what is now Hadley Green in the contrary direction. We can hardly suppose that so experienced a leader would have been unobservant of the depression to the north of Hadley Church, or insensible to the danger of having it in the rear of his position. Besides which, he enjoyed the advantage of being first in the field, and was in a condition, we may presume, to study its features before they became obscured by the fog. This accords moreover with Sir John Paston's statement, when writing to his mother from sanctuary in London on the Thursday following, that the encounter took place 'halfe a mile from Barnet'.

The definition of a plain 0.5 miles from Barnet exactly applies to the situation of the Barnet end of Hadley Green. If one allows for a more generalised somewhere between 0.5 and 1 mile from Barnet, this would place the battle next to the present position of the Hadley Highstone Battle memorial. Also within this space-span lies the moated manor-house of Old Fold, which belonged to the Frowyke family between the thirteenth and fifteenth centuries.

The original manor house is now an eighteenth century replacement, but a large part of the original moat remains, filled with water, behind the Old Fold Golf Club house, next door to the manor house. It may have been an important feature in the conflict; it has been suggested by Warren that it would have made a sensible headquarters for Warwick, being located directly alongside the Great North Road.

Edward ensured that his troops avoided the taverns in Barnet as they marched through. Along with his army, he lodged in the field, having taken up their position in the vicinity of Hadley Green. Cass believes that the eastern end of his position may have been in the immediate vicinity of Hadley Church. Cass states:

> Both armies passed the night under arms, and as we are told by Halle, the tents were so near together that, 'What for neighyng of horses, and talkynge of menne, none of both the hostes could that night take any rest or quietnes.' The result of Edward's disposal of his forces was that, instead of the two armies directly confronting each other, the right of either overlapped its adversary's left. During the night 'Warwick's artillery', in which he was stronger than the King, had been playing from his right wing upon what were believed to be the Yorkist positions in front, but for the reason just stated, the balls fell harmless, no enemy being within the range of this portion of his line of battle. It has also been stated that, though the firing was kept up almost continuously, it did little or no execution, because owing to the nearness of the Yorkists, the shot fell beyond them.

Cass believes that as the foggy day broke around 5 a.m., the battle commenced:

> The Marquis of Montagu, Warwick's brother, with the Earl of Oxford, led the Lancastrian right; the Duke of Somerset commanded the archers in the centre; Warwick in person, with the Duke of Exeter, directed the left. The horses were stationed in either wing. Edward, on his side, seems to have adopted a different formation, and had massed his forces on three lines. His vanguard was commanded by Richard, Duke of Gloucester, who had not long since completed his eighteenth year. Edward himself conducted the battle, in which the captive Henry VI was placed, and Lord Hastings' brought up the rear. He had further a company of fresh men, held in reserve, which eventually did good service. The trumpets now sounded and the battle fairly began. Archers first discharged their arrows and the bill men followed them. For a time, the result of the conflict hung in the balance, and there was an interval when it

Hadley Green is a large open space at the north-west end of Barnet, about 0.5-miles north of Barnet Town if measured from St John's church. The area in the photograph was probably where Warwick made his headquarters. (*Author*)

Old Fold Manor: The original fortified, moated building stood on this site on the original Great North Road, and may well have been Warwick's headquarters. Part of the moat still remains behind the house on the golf course. (*Author*)

The old route of the Great North Road, and approximately 200 yards to the east, the new road. (*Author*)

Old Fold Manor lies behind, to the left of the photograph. The remains of the moat lie filled with water behind the Old Fold Golf Club house, which is behind and to the right. (*Author*)

A stretch of the original Great North Road, 200 yards to the west of the present-day road. The photograph, looking south-north, is taken from outside Old Fold Manor. Old Fold Golf Club, with its moat, is to the left. The western end of Hadley Green, the traditional battle site, is immediately behind the photographer. (*Author*)

seemed more than probable that success would incline to the Lancastrian side. It would appear to have consisted of a succession of engagements or skirmishes over different portions of the field, not directed according to any fixed plan, a result easily accounted for by the obscurity of the weather.

An unexpected incident had an important bearing on the issue of the day. It is not mentioned by Halle, but Stow relates how the Lancastrian right wing, having forced back and routed the left of Edward's position, in returning to resume its place in the line found itself confronted by its own centre. So severe had been their onset that a portion of the Yorkists had been driven through the town, and the report of a Lancastrian victory was carried by certain of the fugitives to London. Halle indeed maintains that they who galloped to London with the intelligence were lookers on and not fighters. Owing, however, to the mist concealing the defeat of Edward's wing, there was no discouragement along the rest of the line.

What happened was that the Earl of Oxford's men scented victory and went into the town of Barnet to loot and pillage. Upon their return to the battlefield, because of the poor visibility, they started to fire on fellow Lancastrians, leading them to believe that they were being betrayed and instigating them to flee from the field. As the chronicler Fabian says, 'If his [Oxford's] men had kept their array and had not fallen to rifling, likely it had been as it was after told that the victory had failed to that party.'

Aftermath and the Death of Warwick

Amongst the Paston family papers survive letters from Sir John Paston, who fought for Henry VI. The letters, sent to his mother at Caistor in Norfolk, describe what had just happened in the battle where he and his younger brother fought on the losing side. The following was written in London on the Thursday of Easter week:

> Mother, recommend me to you, letting you weet, that blessed be God, my brother John is alive and fareth well, and in no peril of death; nevertheless, he is hurt with an arrow in his right arm beneath the elbow; and I have sent him a surgeon, which have dressed him, and he telleth me that he trusteth that he shall be all whole within right short time. It is so that John Mylsent is dead, God have mercy on his soul! [...] There are killed upon the field, half a mile from Barnet, on Easter day, the Earl of Warwick, the Marquis Montague, Sir William Tyrell, Sir Lewis Johns, and diverse other squires of our country, Godmerston, and Booth. And on the King Edward's party, the Lord Cromwell, the Lord Say, Sir Humphrey Bourchier of our country [...] and other people of both parties to the number of more than a thousand.[110]

Warwick and his brother Montague died in the course of the battle. Montagu, according to the *Arrivall*, died 'in playne battayle'. There has been interest in how Warwick died, and versions of events are obscure and various. Warkworth, writing in 1483, says that Warwick, 'Lept on horse-backe and flede to a wode by the felde of Barnett, where was no waye forth...' Subsequently being spotted by a Yorkist soldier, the soldier, '...Came uppone hym and kylled hym, and dispolede him naked.' It was customary in a time of poor communication to quash any rumours that an antagonist may have survived or escaped and thus create a rallying point. Edward thus had the corpses of Warwick and Montagu put in a cart and put naked, with loin cloths, on display at St Pauls before being buried at Bisham Priory in Berkshire. It is likely that they had been born there. During the Reformation, the tombs of Warwick and Montagu were destroyed.[111] Of course, there were more than just the dead. Von Wesel mentions that most of the wounded survivors had been hurt in the lower part of the body and in the face:[112] 'Those who went out with good horses and sound bodies brought home sorry nags and bandaged faces without noses, etc., and wounded bodies, God have mercy on the miserable spectacle.'

The Burial of the Dead

The former battlefield and surrounds conceal the remains of somewhere between 1,500 and 4,000 souls, mostly the remains of the common soldiery. Many of those slain of noble birth were removed to documented burial sites, but as of 2011 we have little more than speculation to say where the remains of the common soldiery are buried. Of the aftermath, Cass cites early sources and says:

> The bodies of the more distinguished amongst the slain on both sides were conveyed away, and many of them interred in the church of the Austin Friars, London. The commonalty, it is stated, were buried on the field, half a mile from Barnet, but no tradition survives as to the spot. Stow informs us that a chapel was erected on the site, and a priest appointed thereto to say mass for their souls. In his time, this chapel had become a dwelling house, of which the top quarters yet remained. It has even been asserted that the church of Hadley was the structure in question, but this is altogether erroneous.

The antiquarian John Weever,[113] writing in 1631, states:

> Most fierce and cruel tells us of burials that on King Edward's side were slain, 'Humphrey Bourchier, Lord Cromwell; Henbry Bourchier, son and heir to the Lord B[e]rners, both buried at Westminster....' Of those fighting for King Henry, he tells us that slain were, 'Richard Nevill, Earl of Warwick, and John Nevill, Marquis Montacute, his brother, both buried in Bisham Abbey in Berkshire. The bodies of many others of the nobility and gentry, on both parties which perished in this unnatural conflict, had Christian burial in the fryar Augustine's church, in London. The common soldiers, as also many commanders, were buried upon the same plain where the foresaid battle was stricken; to whose memory a chapel was built upon the said plain, and a priest appointed to say mass for their souls, as the doctrine went in those days.

We are told in a number of the early accounts that somewhere between 1,000, and 4,000 combatants were killed during the four hours that the battle took place. It is clear from a number of early sources that a chapel was built shortly after the battle for the souls of those that were killed. Brian Warren has looked at the question of the location of the chapel. Fabian's *Great Chronicle of London*, written mainly at the end of the fifteenth century, says, 'In the said playn well upon half a myle from the Town wher' afftyr was byldyud a lytyll Chapell.' A source from *c.* 1589 is more explicit: 'As for the Hermytage it lyeth in the heath; supposed to be builded upon a waste or common belonging to this Mannor: and some wast dooth lye rounde abowt yt. It was (as I am enformed) a chappell wherein the dead bodies were buried in Barnett feilde.'[114] Warren has followed the sequence of references to the chapel or hermitage right through until the 'hermitage' appears on local maps. In 1749, it is shown on land where the business park on Wrotham Park is now located.[115]

Cass, in his history of Monken Hadley, comments that a brass in the knave of Monken Hadley church dated 1442 may commemorate a casualty of the battle.

Dead Man's Bottom in the foreground, facing south towards Barnet, where possibly the dead of the battle were buried. The line of trees on the ridge in the background facing south mark the probable line of the Lancastrian forces, according to the rethinking of the battle site. (*Author*)

The remains of the moated area of the hermitage at the southern end of Wrotham Park. It is likely that the thousands of dead soldiers and their commanders are buried in the immediate vicinity. (*Author*)

Why Cass says this about a brass dated 1442 is unclear. Probably due to structural changes to the floor of the knave, the author was unable to locate the brass when visiting the church in 2010. It also possible that as the battle took place in the vicinity of the church some of the dead may have been buried on the north side of the church, as occurred at St Peters in St Albans.

It is a possibility that the two figures outside the porch on the south side of the church are Edward IV and his queen. It is unlikely though that the rebuilt church, which has the date of 1494 above the main entrance, was the chapel ordered by Edward to commemorate the dead. It is, however, probable that as at other battle sites, such as Towton and St Albans, Hadley Church (St Marys) and St John the Baptist Church in Barnet itself, on the corner of the High Street and Wood Street, were used as a burial places for the fallen.

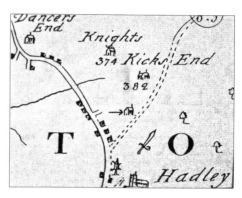

Right: John Warburton's Map of Middlesex 1749 shows the chapel (marked by an arrow) just off the Great North Road.

Below: St Mary the Virgin Church, Monken Hadley, rebuilt in 1494. An earlier church stood here at the time of the battle. (*Author*)

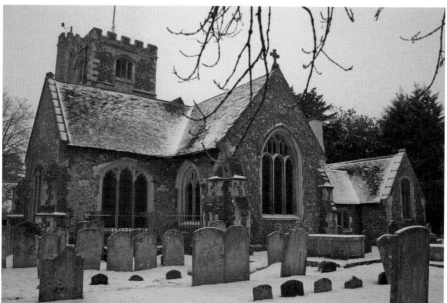

Above and below: The church guide book observes that these two figures outside the porch on the south side may well be the victors of the Battle of Barnet, Queen Elizabeth Woodville (left) and King Edward IV (right). (*Author*)

CHAPTER EIGHT

The Wyatt Rebellion, February 1544

Background

Mary I (1516-1558), often referred to as 'Bloody Mary' on account of her burning 'heretics', was Queen of England from July 1553 until her death in 1558. She was the eldest daughter of Henry VIII and only surviving child of Catherine of Aragon. She was a fanatical Roman Catholic, and succeeded her Protestant half-brother Edward VI. John Dudley, Duke of Northumberland and Edward's chief advisor, had persuaded the dying Edward to exclude his half-sisters Elizabeth and Mary from the line of accession, and attempted to put his Protestant daughter-in-law Lady Jane Grey on the throne. On 10 July 1553, Dudley proclaimed Lady Jane as Queen. Mary raised a force in Suffolk and marched on London. Jane was deposed on 19 July, and her husband, Northumberland's son Guildford Dudley, was seized and placed in the Tower of London. At first, being a Tudor, Mary enjoyed popularity. This, however, diminished when news about her intended marriage to Philip II of Spain leaked out in the autumn of 1553. The Wyatt Rebellion came about in January 1554. The Duke of Suffolk, who had supported Lady Jane Grey, his three brothers, Edward Courtenay, Earl of Devon, and Sir Edmund Warner initiated the Protestant conspiracy. Their prime objective was to replace Mary with Elizabeth and to marry Elizabeth to Edward Courtney. Her reign is mostly remembered for her burning of almost 300 religious dissenters. Her re-establishment of Roman Catholicism was reversed by her successor and half-sister Elizabeth I.

Above left: Edward Courtenay, First Earl of Devon *c.* 1527-1556. He probably instigated the uprising hoping to have married Mary himself.

Above right: Mary (*c.* 1520–1558), also known as 'Bloody Mary', daughter of Henry VIII and a committed Catholic in a now Protestant country. She sparked the uprising when she proposed to marry a foreigner, Phillip II of Spain. (*Hans Eworth*)

Sir Thomas Wyatt

Sir Thomas Wyatt was the son of the poet Sir Thomas Wyatt (1503-1542). His son, also Sir Thomas Wyatt, was born in Allington Castle, Kent, in 1521. Wyatt was hot-headed and impulsive, and without putting proper arrangements in place, was persuaded by Mary's putative husband Edward Courtney to lead a rebellion against Mary I. Wyatt stated it was not his intention to overthrow Mary, but to dissuade Mary from marrying Phillip. In this regard, he led a popular cause.

On 16 November 1553, a formal request was made by a delegation of Parliament to Mary that she should marry an Englishman. One thing the rebels all had in common was their Protestant faith. The date fixed for the rising was 18 March. Wyatt met with close friends at his home Allington Castle and decided that delay was dangerous, as word was spreading of an uprising. The date was changed to 25 January 1554. On market day at Maidstone, Wyatt raised 4,000 men and marched on London.

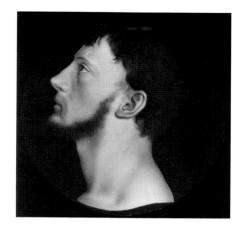

Portrait of Sir Thomas Wyatt the younger.
Beheaded 11 April 1554 on Tower Hill for
leading a rebellion in London against
Mary.

Early Sources

The Wyatt Rebellion is recorded in a number of contemporary and early
histories, including some participant and eye-witness accounts. Probably the two
most interesting accounts, which can both be accessed online, are *The Chronicle
of Queen Jane, and of Two Years of Queen Mary, and especially of the Rebellion of
Sir Thomas Wyat*, edited by John Gough Nichols (Camden Society, 1850), and
also in the Camden Society series and edited by John Gough Nichols, *The diary
of Henry Machyn: Citizen and Merchant-Taylor of London*,[116] which covers the
period between 1550 and 1563. The Chronicle of the Grey Friars of London',
Camden Society old series, volume 53 (1852).

The Uprising Begins

From Henry Machyn's Diary:

> The 26 day of January [...] tidings came to the Queen and her council that sir
> Thomas Wyatt [...] and diverse other gentlemen and commons rose up, and
> they say [it is] because Prince of Spain [is] coming in to have our Queen, for
> they keep Rochester Castle and the bridge and other places.
> The 27 day of January, the City sent into Kent a great number of men in white
> coats. [In other words, a militia to fight Wyatt.] The captains to command
> them, and the rest of their forces, were the Duke of Norfolk, Earl of Ormond,
> Sir George Howard, and divers others. But many of the guards [...] the white-
> coats, deserted them, and [the] captains came home again. [Wyatt had gotten
> some of the late King's] ordnance; and so, after their removing, came towards
> Dartford with his army towards London.

Holinshed's chronicle of 1586 tells us that Wyatt and 10,000 men reached Greenwich on Friday 2 February, and on the Saturday he was seen by observers in the Tower of London marching with a vanguard of around 2,000 men towards London Bridge, with a number of guns. At this point, Mary's troops stationed at St George's Church in Southwark retired to the London Bridge, where they destroyed the draw-bridge and set up fortifications on the bridge, which included 'great ordnance' or cannon.[117]

Dromes [drums] went thorough London at iiij of the clocke, warning all soldears to arme themselves and to repaire to Charing crosse. The queene was once determined to come to the Tower forthwith, but shortelie after she sende worde she would tarry ther to see the uttermost. Many thought she wolde have been in the fielde in person.

Here was no small a-dowe [ado] in London, and likewise the Tower made great preparation of defence. By ten of the clocke, or somewhat more, the Earle of Pembroke had set his troop of horsemen on the hill in the highway above the new bridge over against Saynt James; his footemen was sett in two Battailles [battalions] somewhat lower, and nearer Charing crosse. At the lane turning downe by the bricke wall from Islington-warde he had sett also certain other horsemen, and he had planted his ordenance upon the hill side. In the meane season Wyat and his company planted his ordenance upon the hill beyond Saynt James, almost over against the park corner; and himself, after a fewe words spoken to his soldears [...] And so came the daye toward Saynt James fielde, where as was the Earle of Pembroke, the Queens leftenant, and my Lord privy seal [the Earl of Bedford], and my Lord Paget, and my Lord Clynton, which was Lord Marshall of the campe, with divers other lords on horseback; which Lord Clynton ghawe [gave] the charge with the horsemen by the [Hyde] parke corner, which was about twelve of the clocke that daye, and Wyat so passed hym selve with a smalle company, towards Charryng crosse, and so towards Fle[e]t streate, &c.

From Henry Machyn's Diary[118]

The same day [1 February] at afternoon was a proclamation in Cheapside, Leadenhall, and at saint Magnus corner, with herald of arms and [...] the Queen['s] trumpeters blowing, and my Lord Mayor, and my Lord Admiral Howard, and the two sheriffs, that sir Thomas Wyatt was proclaimed traitor and rebellious, and all his fellows, against the Queen['s] majesty and her counsel, and that he would have the Queen in custody, and the Tower of London in keeping; and they conveyed unto every gate guns and the bridge; and so every gate with men in harness [armour] night and days. And about three of the clock at afternoon the Queen['s] grace came riding from Westminster unto Guild-hall with many lords, knights, and ladies, and bishops and heralds of arms, and trumpeters blowing and all the guard in harness. [Then she declared, in an oration to the mayor and the city, and to her council, her mind concerning her marriage, that she never intended to marry out of her realm but by her council's consent and advice; and that she would never marry but all her true] subjects shall be content, [or else she would live] as her grace has done hitherto. But that her grace will call a parliament [as] shortly as [may be, and] as they shall find, and that [the Earl of] Pembroke shall be chief captain and general against Sir Thomas Wyatt and his fellows in the [field,] that my lord admiral for to be [in associate] with the [Lord Mayor] to keep the city from all-comers thereto. [After this] the Queen['s] grace came from Guild-hall [...] and took her barge [to] Westminster to her own place the same day.

The third day of February was a proclamation that who so ever do take sir Thomas Wyatt [...] should have £100 land to him and his heirs for ever.

The third day of February came in to Southwark Sir Thomas Wyatt and other captains at after-noon with his army; and the morow after they made trenches in diverse parts and diverse places with ordnance.

On the Saterday [4 February] folowing very early, Wyat marched to Southwarke, where approching the gate at London bridge foote, called to them with in to have it opened, which he found not so readie as he looked for.

Wyat yet adventured the breaking downe of a wall out of a house ioyning to the gate at the bridge foote, Sir Thomas Wyat's desperate attempt whereby he might enter into the leades over the gate, came downe into the lodge about xj of the clocke in the night, where he found the porter in a slumber, and his wife with other waking, and watching over a cole, but beholding Wyat, they began sodainly to start as greatly amazed. Whift quoth Wyat, as you love your lyves sit still, you shall have no hurt. Glad were they of that warrãt, and so were quiet and made no noyse.

Stowe, in his *Annals*, tells us that the lieutenant of the tower, that same night, in revenge for one of his boatmen who had been shot by Wyatt's men:

Sent seaven great pieces of ordnance, culverings,[199] and demi-canons, full against the foot of the [London] Bridge, and against Southwarke, and the two steeples of St Olaves[120] and Saint Mary Overies, besides all the pieces on the White Tower, one culvering on the Diveling Tower,[121] and three fauconets[122] over the Water-gate.[123]

Machyn's diary for the Shrove Tuesday tells us:

The sixth day of Feybruary was Shrove Tuesday [...] In the morning, master Wyat and his company returned back toward Kingston upon Thames, and

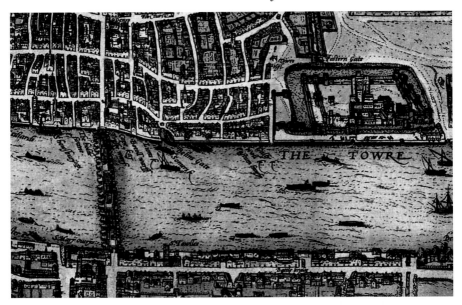

Braun and Hogenberg 1572 Map of London, illustrating the field of fire between St Mary Overies (Southwark Cathedral) and the tower, with London Bridge in between.

there the bridge was plucked up, and he caused one of his men to swim over for to fetch a boat, and so went at night toward Kensington, and so forward.

The same day was two hanged upon a gibbet in Paul's churchyard; the one a spy of Wyat, the other was under-sheriff of Leicester, for carrying letters of the Duke of Suffolk and other things.

The same day came riding to the tower the Duke of Suffolk and his brother the Earl of Huntington with 300 horse.

Holinshed elaborates and tells us that when Wyatt marched the 10 miles to Kingston, they reached the next available bridge for crossing the Thames:

They [Wyatt and his men] arryved [at Kingston] about foure of the Clocke in the after Noone, and finding thirtie foote or there aboute of the Bridge taken away, saving the Postes that were left standing, Wyat practised wyth two Mariners to swimme over, and to convey a barge to him, which the Mariners through great promises of preferment accordingly did, wherein Wiat and certaine with him were conveyed over, who in the meane time that the number of the souldiours based in the towne, caused the Bridge to be repaired with ladders, plankes, and beames, Wyat repayreth the bridge [...] at Kingston the same being tied together with Ropes and Boardes so as by tenne of the clocke in the night, it was in such plight, that both his Ordinaunce, and companyes of men might passe over wythout perill & so about xj of the clocke in the same night, Wiat with his army passing over ye bridge withoute either resystance or perill, and before it coulde bee once knowne at the Court, marched towardes London, meaning (as some have written) to have beene at the Court gate before day that morning: neverthelesse before hee came within six myles of the Citie, Grafton, The Earle of Pembroke in order staying uppon a peece of his greate artillerie, whiche was dismounted by the way, his coming was discovered before day, whereby the Earle of Pembrooke being Generall of the Queenes armie (as is before sayde) was with his men in good order of battaile in Saint Iames fielde besyde Westminster, two or three houres before Wyat could reache thyther.

The Spanish Ambassador, who was advising Mary, sums up in his despatches to Spain the tense atmosphere at court, and the fear felt by Mary and those around her:

He [Wyatt] got all his men across during the night and approached this town, coming up to within six miles of Westminster and St James, which so frightened the Council that they went to the Queen between two and three o'clock of the morning to urge her to get up and fly by boat. She, without losing her presence of mind for an instant, sent for me. Now, the day before, the Chancellor had spoken much about Courtenay's evil doings and advised the Queen to go to Windsor, whereupon she had commanded me to tell her whether I thought it would be wise to withdraw. I told her that unless she wished to lose her kingdom, she by no means ought to do so while any force or expedient remained to be tried. If London rose, the Tower would be lost, the heretics would throw religious affairs into confusion and kill the priests, Elizabeth would be proclaimed Queen, irremediable harm would be the result, and I could not advise her to depart without more urgent cause. So at the said hour of the morning when I appeared before her I repeated the same opinion, and she repeated it to her Council, several members of which, and especially the Chancellor, were greatly perturbed and urged her to depart, whilst others opposed the notion. At last, she summoned up her courage and decided not to go if Lords Pembroke and Clinton did their duty, to whom she at once sent off a messenger, and they replied imploring her not to move and assuring her that God would give her the victory.[124]

Fighting at Hyde Park and St James's Park

Wyatt and his men, doubling back towards London from Kingston, approached London via Brentford and Knightsbridge. Machyn tells us:

[On] the seventh day of February, in the forenoon, Wyatt, with his army and ordnance, were at Hyde Park Corner. There the Queen's host met with a great number of men at arms on horseback, beside foot. By one of the clock the Queen['s and Wyatt's men had a skirmish;] there were many slain; butt master Wyatt took the way down by Saint James with a great company and so to Charing Cross, and so forth, crying 'God save queen Mary!' till he came to Ludgate and [knocked there; thinking to have entered; but the gate being kept fast against him, he retired,] and backe agayne unto Temple Bar, and folowed hym many men, and ther he yielded unto master Norray the herald of armes in his cote of armes, and ther he lycted behynd a gentleman unto the courte; but by the way many of them were slayne by the way or thay came to Charyng-crosse, what with mores pykes and bylls; and many of Wyatt['s] men, as they whent, wher the queens friendes and Englishmen under a false pretense [...] the queen['s] grace had given them pardon; and dyvers of his men tooke the queen['s] men by the hand as thay whent toward Ludgaet. Thys was done on As-Wedynsday, the furst yere of Queen Mary of England; and the sam nyght to the Towre Sir Thomas Wyatt, Master Cobham, and Master Vane, and ij Knewetes and odur captaynes.

State Papers

So with all speed, all her forces of horse and foot were gathered together, trenches were dug, artillery put in position, infantry above 1,000 strong was drawn up, and three good squadrons of cavalry were formed to wait for Wyatt. He, not thinking the Queen's forces to be so strong, and expecting the conspirators and heretics to rise like desperate men in his support, started on a disorderly march towards St James' and reached town with 400 men. The Queen's cavalry routed the other rebels, taking 400 or 500 prisoners and wounding as many again. Wyatt was captured at the city gate, and all his captains were killed or taken.

Wyatt, with only around sixty men left, retreated from Ludgate, where he had failed to gain entry. He entered the courtyard of the Belle Sauvage Inn, which was maybe 300 yards distant. From there, he decided to retreat to Charing Cross with around sixty men. He got as far as Temple Bar, where he surrendered to a herald. The Wyatt Rebellion was over.

The Spanish Ambassador reports:

Courtenay and the Earl of Worcester showed no sign of fighting, and distinguished themselves on this their first field by running off to Court crying that all was lost and the rebels were winning the day [...] The Queen is angered and intends to consult with the Council as to what shall be done with him and Elizabeth, who is fortifying herself in her house, where she is lying ill. There is news that she now uses in a week the same quantity of victuals that used to last her a month.

The same day, the Queen received a report of the capture of my Lord Thomas, second brother of the Duke of Suffolk, and also that Crofts had been taken.

The Duke of Suffolk has written out with his own hand and signed his confession, in which he owns that irritation at his arrest, the small esteem in which the Council held him, his alarm when Warner was arrested, and the conversation of Carew and Crofts, who had plotted, together with many others, to set the Lady Elizabeth on the throne, moved him to leave the Queen's party and join the rebels. His brother Thomas, he says, specially strove to persuade him, and also tried to win over Pembroke, who refused to listen. And he implores mercy, not justice. Thomas, who is a prisoner, has also written begging the Queen to have pity, but she is resolved to let justice have its course, as her clemency has already been abused, and allow their heads to be cut off.

Bringing a chilling immediacy to his report, the Ambassador reports of Mary: 'If her commands were executed last Tuesday, Jane of Suffolk (Lady Jane Grey) and her husband were to have lost their heads on that day, but I am not certain that the deed has yet been done.'[125]

The Immediate Aftermath

It is clear that Mary and her court were by no means confident that Wyatt could be overcome, or that the citizens of London would not rise up against her. There survives a report by one of the Queen's guard, who happens to be a Protestant, of what happened inside the court at St James's Palace.[126] When some soldiers wanted to open the gate to go and confront Wyatt, the Queen agreed to have the gates opened, but the envoy from the Queen, who was in the gallery, was told:

Yow wyll not goo far off her sight, for her only trust is in yow for the defence of her parsone this daye. So the gate was opened, and we marched before the galary wyndowe, where she spake unto us, requyrynge us, as we weare jentyllmen in whome she only trusted, that we wolde nott goo from that place. Ther we marched upe and downe the space off an ower, and then came a herald [...] to bring newes that Wyatt was taken.

The relief at court is evident. The writer says that they were all taken into Mary's presence, where 'every one kissed her hande, off whome we hadde greate thanks, and large promises how goode she wolde be unto us; but fewe or none off us got any thynge, although she was very liberall to many others that weare enemys unto God's worde, as fewe off us weare.' From the state papers we learn:

> Immediately after the battle was won, the Earl of Pembroke and all the lords and gentlemen came to announce the good news to the Queen, who thanked them in terms so appropriate that they all fell to weeping. She dwelt on the gratuitous wrong Wyatt had done in conspiring against her crown and realm under the pretext of her marriage, which she had decided upon for her kingdom's good, as they, most of whom had advised her to do so, well knew. Then, in Courtenay's presence, she gave Pembroke a diamond as a token of her gratitude and promise to remember his services, whereat all cried 'long live the Queen!' and swore to live and die her servants. After this, Wyatt was taken off to prison and the Queen desired to see him from one of her windows. To-day his trial is being held, so that he may be executed as soon as possible.[127]

Henry Machyn

> The eighth day of February was commanded by the Queen and the Bishop of London that [St] Pauls and every Parish that they should sing Te Deum Laudamus, and ringing for the good victory that the Queen['s] grace had against Wyatt and the rebellious of Kent, the which were over-come, thanks be unto God, with little blood-shed, and the residue taken and had to prison, and after were divers of them put to death in divers places in London and Kent.

Bloody Revenge

Mary's revenge was swift. Many of the key parts of the city and many points outside, such as Hyde Park Corner, the Strand, Fleet Street, Hay Hill, and Holborn, had gallows erected in order that the consequences of the uprising could be observed by ordinary Londoners. Those who defected to Wyatt in the beginning, the 'white coats', paid a heavy price. Holinshed tells us:

> Poore capytifs were brought forth, being so many in number, that all the prisons in London sufficed not to receive them, so that for lacke of place, they were faine to bestowe them in diverse Churches of the sayde Citie; and shortly after were set up in London for a terrour to the common sort, (bycause the

white coates beeing sent out of the Citie (as before ye have heard) revolted from the Queenes parte, to the aide of Wyat) twentie payre of Gallowes, on the which were hanged in severall places to the number of fiftie perfons, which Gallowes remayned standing there a great part of the Sommer following, to the greate griefe of good Citizens, and for example to the Commitioners.[128]

Henry Machyn is more specific as to the locations of the gallows set up in London:

The twelfth day of February was made at every gate in London a new pair of gallows and set up, two pair in Cheapside, two pair in Fleet Street, one in Smithfield, one pair in Holborn, one at Leaden-hall, one at saint Magnus London [-Bridge], one at Pepper Alley gate, one at Saint Georges [Southwark], one in Barunsaystret, one on Tower hill, one pair at Charing Cross, one pair beside Hyde Park corner.

The fourteenth day of February were hanged at every gate and place: in Cheapside six; Aldgate one, quartered; at Leadenhall three; at Bishopsgate one, and quartered Moorgate one; Cripplegate one; Aldersgate one, quartered Newgate one, quartered Ludgate one; Billingsgate three hanged; Saint Magnus three hanged; Tower hill two hanged; Holborn three hanged; Fleet Street three hanged; at Pepper alley gate three; Barunsaystret three; Saint Georges three; Charing cross four [...] at Hyde park corner three, on Polard a waterbearer; theyre three hangs in chains; and but seven quartered, and their bodies and heads set upon the gates of London.

The sixteenth day of February was made a great scaffold in Westminster hall for the Duke of Suffolk.

The seventeenth day of February was the Duke of Suffolk arraigned at Westminster Hall, and cast for the treason, and cast to suffer death.

Henry Grey, Duke of Suffolk, was the father of Lady Jane Grey. The uprising had convinced Mary that it was now too dangerous to allow Lady Jane Grey and her husband Gilbert Dudley to remain alive in the tower. Therefore, on 12 February both she and her husband were executed. Five days after Jane's execution, Suffolk was brought to trial and found guilty of treason for his part in Dudley's scheme. He was beheaded on Tower Hill on 23 Feb 1554.[129] *The Chronicles of the Grey Friars of London* report:

Item the xij of February was beheddyd wythin the tower Lady Jane that woulde a beene Qweene; and hare husband whose name was Gylford Dudley at the Tower-hyll.

Item the xiiij day of the same monyth for the same rebellyon was hangyd one vicars, a yeoman of the guarde, Bouthe one of the Queenes footmen, gret John Nortone, and one Kynge; and in severalle places abowte London at the gattes, in Chappe syde [Cheapside] and other streettes, to the number of xxti, the wych ware of London that fled from the duke of Norfoke; and that same day was iij hangyd in chanys on Hay hylle for the offence in rebellyon.[130]

Wyatt's Fate

Wyatt was imprisoned in the White Tower, where he remained while he was tortured and attempts were made by the authorities to implicate Mary's half-sister Elizabeth in the plot. He witnessed the execution of Lady Jane Grey just six days before his own execution on 11 April.

The contemporary *Chronicle of Queen Jane* describes Wyatt's final day:

An hower and more. What was spoken is not yet knowen. Then he was brought out with a boke [...] The xith of Aprell, being wenysdaye, was sir Thomas Wyat beheded upon Tower-hill. Before his coming downe out of the Tower, the Lorde Chamberlayne and the Lorde Shandos caryed him to the tower over the Watergaste, wher the Lorde Courtney laye, and ther he was before Courtney half in his hande; and at the garden pale the Lord Chamberlayne tooke his leave of him, and likewise master secretarye Bourne, to whom master Wyat said: 'I praie you, sir, pray for me, and be a meane to the queen for my poor wife anmd children; and yf yt might have pleased her grace to have granted me my lyfe I would have trusted to have don hir such good service as shold have well recompenced myne offence; but since not, I besech God have mercy on me.' To which Master Bourne made no answer. So he came toward the [Tower] hill, Weston leading him by one arme and the Lord Shandose by the other. When he was uppe apon the scaffold he desired eche man to praye for him and with him and said these or moche-like words in effecte: 'Good people, I am come presently here to dye, being thereunto lawfully and wourthely condemned, for I have sorely offended against God and the Quenes majestie, and I am sorry therefore. I trust God hath forgiven and taken his mercy upon me. I besyche the Queens majesty also of forgevenes.' 'She hath forgiven you allredy,' saith Weston. 'And let every man beware howe he taketh eny thinge in hande against the higher powers [...] And I pray God I may be the last example in this place for that or eny other like. And whereas yt is said and wysled abroade, that I should accuse my Lady Elizabeth's grace, and my Lorde Courtney; yt is not so, goode people, for I assure you neyther they nor eny other now.' And whether Mr Wyat, being the amased at such interruption, or whether they on the scaffold pluct him by the gown bake or no, yt is not well knowen, but without more talk he tourned him, and put of his gown and untrussyd his pointes, then, taking the [Earl of] Huntingdon, the Lorde Hastinges, Sir Giles Stranguesh, and many other by the hands, he plucked of his doblet and wastcote, unto his shirte, and knelyd downe upon the strawe, then laied his hed downe awhile, and rayse on his knees again, then after a few wourdes spoken, and his eyes lyft upp to heaven, he knytt the handekersheve himself about his eyes, ad a lyttel holding upp his hands suddenly laid downe his hed, which the hangeman at one stroke toke from him. Then was he forthwith quarteryd apon the scaffold, and the next day his quarters set at diverse places, and his hed apon a stake apon the gallos beyond saynte James. Which his hed, as ys reported, remained not there x dayes unstolne awaye.[131]

Wyatt was thirty-three years old when he died. His quartered body was then displayed in Newington, Mile End Green, St Georges Church, Southwark,[132] besides St Thomas of Waterings.[133] His head was placed on a pole at Hay Hill.[134] On 17 April, his head was stolen and never recovered.

The Beheading Sr Thos Wyatt.

An early depiction of Sir Thomas Wyatt's execution on Tower Hill.

CHAPTER NINE

The Battles of Brentford and Turnham Green, 12 and 13 November 1642

English Civil War Background

The civil war was a conflict over which party had the right to rule the country: King, Parliament, or both in conjunction with each other. King Charles I believed that he was monarch by divine right. The Royal Standard was raised on 22 August 1642. The war that followed split the kingdom, with some families fighting each other. The nobility likewise fought as readily for Parliament as for the King, and changing sides was not uncommon. Picking the losing side could lead to confiscation of estates, and in many cases, execution. Brentford, 8-miles west of London, at this time was a small 'mean' one street town, situated on the Thames and the route into and out of London to the west. In November 1642, the town had been prepared to stand in the way of King Charles and his nephew Prince Rupert. On 23 October, after the Battle of Edgehill, the King's army, under Rupert, captured Banbury, Oxford, Abingdon, Aylesbury, and Maidenhead. Windsor was too strong to take, but Rupert wanted to continue to London. The commander of the Parliamentary army, the Earl of Essex, managed to overtake Rupert, and he arrived in London with his army by 8 November. Charles remained in Reading, and agreed to open negotiations with Parliament, but felt that if he moved closer to London it would strengthen his hand. There were some negotiations that led Parliament to believe that there would be a peaceful settlement.[138]

Charles then marched his army to Colnbrook on 11 November and told Rupert to take nearby Brentford. A letter was sent from Parliament to the King, assuming he was still at Colnbrook, but:

> In fact, Charles and his army were already on the move. Before sunrise, the Royalist soldiers quartered around Colnbrook, Longford [... and] readied

The Parliamentary Captain-General was Robert Devereux, 3rd Earl of Essex (1591-1646), who commanded the Parliamentarian army for the first three years of the Civil War.

themselves to march on the capital [...] when it was on Hounslow Heath the royal army was halted and deployed into battle formation [...] They resumed the advance across Hounslow Heath, through the village of Hounslow, towards Brentford, 2 miles away, which had been the objective since the previous day.[135]

Brentford 1642

Brentford in 1642 was a small town with about 280 houses, and a population of around 1,500. It was a busy market town built along the Great West Road. The town was a river port, 'With wharves on the Brent, close to its confluence with the Thames. The town had developed a somewhat sleazy reputation, as a place frequented by Londoners carrying on illicit liaisons, because of its inns and its proximity to the city.'[136]

It was its position that gave it importance, in that it had a stone bridge over the River Brent, which was a natural defensive position. It was also in a key position along the east-west route in and out of London, 8 miles to the east. An early map of Brentford, the Moses Glover's 1635 Map of Brentford (see illustration), shows a largely rural but enclosed aspect of the countryside around the town. The predominance of hedges made it likely that the engagement would have involved mainly concealed cannons, muskets, and the use of infantry.

The 1635 plan, which is looking from the town to the west, shows Sir Richard Wynn's House (top centre) where the fighting began.[137] The still standing church of St Lawrence (centre left), where some burials took place, can be seen, along with Syon House, home of Algernon Percy, Earl of Northumberland, where fighting also took place. Wynn's House, built in the image of nearby Syon House, was demolished in the nineteenth century. All that remains is the nearby 'Lion Gate' and open land, which looks south-easterly towards Syon House.

Extract from the Rocque 1745 Map of Brentford. Clearly visible is Syon House, Brentford High Street, with the islands just off the shore, Brentford Bridge, St Lawrence's Church in outline, and slightly to the north-east of the bridge, the Butts.

Brentford Prepares

There was concern that the King's commander Prince Rupert might use his base to march on and pillage London. The Earl of Essex took control of the bridge at Kingston upon Thames, and set up a barricade at the west end of Brentford, in the vicinity of the bridge that connected Old Brentford to New Brentford. On 11 November, there were negotiations between Parliament's representatives and the King at Colnbrook, but the King had already decided to march on London the next day. Also, Denzil Holles and Lord Brooke's 'parliamentarian regiments of foot had arrived in Brentford by the morning of 11 November. They were short of arms, match, bullet, and powder, and [they] ransacked the shops in the town for supplies.'[138]

The Battle

The battle that followed has been described as a running skirmish that ran through the length of town. The day started off foggy. The survival of so many participant accounts allows a fairly full reconstruction of what took place. John Gwyn was a soldier in Sir Thomas Salisbury's (royalist) regiment of foot, and he relates the attack on Sir Richard Wynn's house:[139]

> The very first day that five comrades of us repaired from the Court at Richmond to the King's royal army, which we met accidentally that morning upon Hounslow Heath, we had no sooner put ourselves into rank and file, under the command of our worthy old acquaintance Sir George Bunckley [then Major to Sir Thomas Salusbury], but we marched up to the enemy, engaged them by Sir Richard Winn's house and the Thames side, beat them to retreat into Brainford, beat them from one Brainford to the other, and from thence to the open field, with a resolute and expeditious fighting, that after firing suddenly to advance up to push of pikes and butt end of muskets [...] that abundance of them were killed and taken prisoners, besides those drowned in their attempts to escape by leaping into the river.

The route that John Gwyn took would have been an 'advance from the south, through Isleworth along Syon Lane and perhaps alongside the Thames [...] An orchard covering 15 acres lay between Syon House and the Brent, which could have provided parties of Royalist skirmishers with cover to approach the road through Brentford End'.[140]

Attack at Brentford Bridge

The bridge and banks of the River Brent had been barricaded by the Parliamentarian troops who waited behind the barricades. The first Royalist attempt to storm the bridge using cavalry failed, due to the heavy fire from concealed cannon. The second attempt by foot regiments also failed, at which point the Royalists brought up more reinforcements and stormed the bridge again.[141] Sir Richard Bulstrode served in the Prince of Wales' regiment of horse. He initially describes the approach to the bridge:[142]

> At first, we found considerable opposition. The Prince of Wales's regiment of Horse, where I was, being drawn up behind a great hedge, where the enemy had planted some cannon, which we saw not till they played so fast upon us that we lost some men and were obliged to draw off and retire for our better security; and upon our foot's coming up, we beat the regiments of Hambden and Hollis out of the town, took several prisoners and arms, and sunk two great barks in the river Thames with many soldiers; Parliamentarians started to fall back 'from the one Brainford to the other, and from thence to the open field'.[143]

The Lion Gate on the Great West Road marks the approximate position where the fighting began. Brentford Town and the bridge over the River Brent is about 0.5 mile to the left. (*L. Abrahams*)

Another Royalist soldier, Matthew Smallwood, has left an account of what happened next:[144]

> We went to Hounslow towne, thence to Brainford, where unexpectedly we were encountered by two or three regiments of theirs, who had made some small barricadoes [barricades] at the end of the first towne called New Brainford. The van of our army being about 1,000 musketiers, answered their shot soe bitterly that within an hour or lesse, they foresooke their work in that place and fled up to another which they had raised betwixt the two townes, from whence and a brick house by with two small ordnance they gave us a hot and long shower of bullets. My Colonel's [Sir Edward Fitton] regiment was the sixth that was brought to assault, after five others had all discharged, whose happy honour it was (assisted by God and a good pair of cannon newly come up) to drive them from that worke too, where it was an heart-breaking object to hear and see the miserable deaths of many goodly men.
>
> We slew a lieutenant-colonel, 2 serjeant-majors, some captains and others, officers and soldiers there about 30 or 40 of them, took 400 prisoners. But what was most pitiful was to see how many poore men ended and lost there lives striving to save them, for they ran into the Thames, about 200 of them, as we might judge, were drowned by themselves and so were guilty of their own deaths; for had they stayed, and yielded up themselves, the King's mercy is so

Brentford Bridge viewed west-east. The church tower can be seen between the traffic lights to the right. Fierce fighting took place here when the Prince of Wales' regiment of horse attempted to storm the bridge, but failed due to fire from concealed cannon. The Battlefield Trust have a 'what happened here' information board by the bridge. (*Author*)

The banks of the River Brent were barricaded by the Parliamentarian forces as well as the bridge itself. (*Author*)

gracious that he had spared them all. We took there 6 or 8 colours, also their two pieces of ordnance, and all this with very small losse. God be praised, for believe me, I cannot understand that we lost 16 men, whereof, one was a sone of Mr Daniel of Tabley, Mr Thomas Daniel, a fine young gentlemen (who was a Lieutenant under my Lord Rivers). He and his captain were both slain, and a lieutenant in our regiment, but none of our countrymen. Then we thinking all had been done for that night, two of our regiments marched up through the old towne to make good the entrance, but they were again encountered by a fresh onset which scattered like the rest, after a short conflict, fled away towards Hammersmith and we were left masters of the towne.

Fighting at Syon House

Matthew Smallwood continues his account on how, having secured the town, they slept in the cold fields the night of 11 November. Syon House was probably treated lightly by both sides for fear of alienating Northumberland, who it has been suggested could influence a peaceful settlement.[145] There is no doubt that the house was involved in the fighting and sustained some minor damage:

> The household accounts for 1643 record repairs, costing £26 10s, where the house had been shot through with ordnance, the battlements damaged, and the 'three ovals in the middle gallery […] which were shot through by the King's forces'. While this is a clear reference to the events of November 1642, it is uncertain whether the damage to the gallery refers to Royalist forces firing into the house as part of an attempt to dislodge parliamentarian troops at some point on 12 November, or in an exchange of fire on the following day. There is some confusion over the timing of the blowing up of barges: '…On 13 November…' According to a Parliamentarian pamphlet, on that afternoon, two pinnaces,[146] deployed by Parliament to prevent the Royalists using boats to land forces at Whitehall or in the City, attacked Syon House with cannon, damaging it substantially. The Royalist counter-fire, from cannon on the 'top' of the house and 'lower', was largely ineffective; the former apparently because it overshot the ships and the latter because it was inconvenient to use, possibly because of the heavy, rain-sodden nature of the ground. However, one of the vessels was sunk by Royalist fire, according to the pamphlet, due to the skill of the King's engineers.[147]

Smallwood tells us:

> Next morning early we were started afresh by the loud music of some cannon, which proved to be some 14 barges of theirs, who with 13 ordnance and 600 men attempted (very indifferently) to pass up the river from Kingston, by the town where we lay,

to London, but being discovered, what from the bancke and from Sion House [the Earl of Northumberland's] where we had placed some four musketiers, within two or three howers space we sunk four or five of their vessels with the canons in them, took the rest, and three pieces in them for our breakfast. After which, within two hours we could descry a great army marching downe upon us from London, who came up within musket shot of us, but the King finding his men wearie and being satisfied with what he had done before for that tyme, and having no convenient room for his horse (which is the greatest pillar of his army) to fight, very wisely drew of his men by degrees and unperceived by them leaves the towne naked, some of his horse dragooners keeping them deceived till the foot were all gone and then galloped in the rear. After which, the enemy perceiving played on their back with their cannon, but with no harmful success at all, God be praised. Soe that night we marched back towards Hampton Court, next day to Kingston, a great towne which they had manned the day before with 6,000 men in it, but left it upon our fight at Brainford. So here we are now very safe, our foot and our horse about us. And so you have a brief report of what these days have brought forth.

The Royalists were victorious, but their army was delayed by the Parliamentarian resistance and halted outside the town at nightfall. This allowed the Parliamentary field army and London militia to form-up on Turnham Green and halt the King's advance on London the next day.

Sacking of Brentford

Looting was a given part of warfare. The day before battle, the Parliamentarians had raided the town for their needs, and after his victory, Rupert allowed his troops to ravage Brentford. Prince Rupert had already been condemned by the Parliamentarians and the London press 'as a rapacious soldier who would bring the dreadful and destructive practices of the Thirty Years War into England'. There were pamphlets being distributed that showed Rupert on horseback with his poodle 'boy', a pistol, and Birmingham behind him in flames.[148]
Rupert's soldiers:

Went on the rampage in the town of Old Brentford [...] They took from the inhabitants their Money, Linnen, Woollen, Bedding, Horses, Cows, Swine, Hens, etc., and all manners of victuals. Also, Pewter, Brasses, Iron Pots and Kettles [...] They did cut in pieces and burn the poor Fishermen's Boats and Nets by which they got their living [...] And when they had taken away all the Goods (except here and there a Bed), they defaced some houses and set one on fire.

The damage was estimated to be £ 4,000.

Syon House, home at that time of Algernon Percy, Earl of Northumberland and nominally a Parliamentarian, had been captured by Royalists, and according to household accounts of 1643, was damaged in the fighting.

Above left: Memorial outside Brentford County Court on the main road through Brentford recording three campaigns: 51 BC Julius Caesar, AD 910 Edmund Ironside's defeat of Cnut, and in 1642, 'Close by was fought the Battle of Brentford…' (*Author*)

Above right: The burial registers for St Lawrence, New Brentford, for November and December 1642 list six officers 'and divers others which were slain'. One of these was a Royalist soldier. Their burial ground is, in 2011, derelict, and the church premises are for sale. (*Author*)

What Remains?

Much of seventeenth century Brentford has disappeared under development. The Butts where the Parliamentarian cavalry was stationed remain, but with later seventeenth and eighteenth century buildings, and signposts from the High Street. The area of the Butts retains much by way of atmosphere.

St Lawrence's Church has been rebuilt, but the tower is original and pre-dates the battle. Unfortunately, the church is decaying and derelict. The bridge over the River Brent has been replaced twice since 1642. A local historian has observed:

> Boston Manor House[149] is the only building to remain from Civil War days. According to local legend, it was from here that King Charles watched the battle. He may also have been in the house during the stand-off at Turnham Green; he is known to have offered peace talks in Brentford during that day and Boston Manor House would have been the most likely setting.[150]

Of actual cannon balls and musket shot little has been found, although *Brentford Past* mentions:

> Cannon balls in the collection of the Museum of London are alleged to be relics of the Battle of Brentford, and a report in *The Times* newspaper of 1883 tells us that 'a large number of antiquated horse shoes of various shapes' were discovered at a depth of 8 feet during excavations for Brentford's new sewerage system. Some were surrounded with calcareous matter, suggesting the presence of decayed bones. At the time, it was suggested these were shoes from horses killed in the Brentford battle; they may have been, although a more prosaic, but more likely explanation is that the excavators had stumbled on the premises of an early blacksmith.[151]

Dealing with the Dead

The reality of Brentford was that the battle lasted but a short time and the numbers involved were, as was common in warfare, exaggerated or minimised by both sides for propaganda purposes. As Gillian Clegg[152] observes, the range varies from the Venetian ambassador's estimate that the Parliamentarians lost 2,000 men, to other, more realistic estimates that put the number at between 10 and 60.

The Battlefield Trust tells us:

> The burial registers of St Lawrence's Church, Brentford, for November and December 1642 record the burials of two Parliamentary captains and three lieutenants. The most senior Parliamentary officer at Brentford, Lieutenant

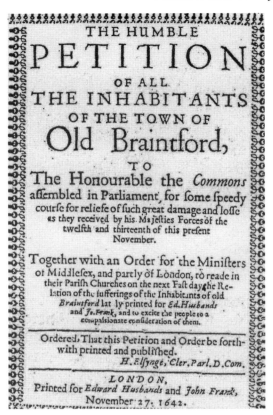

THE HUMBLE
PETITION
OF ALL
THE INHABITANTS
OF THE TOWN OF
Old Braintford,

TO

The Honourable the *Commons*
aſſembled in Parliament, for ſome ſpeedy
courſe for reliefe of ſuch great damage and loſſe
as they received by his Majeſties Forces of the
twelfth and thirteenth of this preſent
November.

Together with an Order for the Miniſters
of Middleſex, and partly of London, to reade in
their Pariſh Churches on the next Faſt dayghe Relation of the ſufferings of the Inhabitants of old
Braintford lat ly printed for *Ed.Husbands*
and *Jo.Frank*, and to excite the people to a
compaſſionate conſideration of them.

Ordered, That this Petition and Order be forthwith printed and publiſhed.
H. Elſynge, Cler.Parl.D.Com.

LONDON,
Printed for *Edward Husbands* and *John Frank*,
November 27. 1642.

A petition dated two weeks after Prince Rupert's men pillaged Brentford requesting assistance from Parliament. Parliament would have seen this as good anti-Royalist propaganda.

Colonel James Quarles of Lord Brooke's regiment of foot, is mentioned in an eye-witness source as having been killed.

Matthew Smallwood, writing four days later, gives us an idea of the numbers involved:

It was a heart-breaking object to hear and see the miserable deaths of many goodly men. We slew a lieutenant-colonel, 2 serjeant-majors, some captains and others, officers and soldiers there about 30 or 40 of them, took 400 prisoners. But what was most pitiful was to see how many poore men ended and lost there lives striving to save them, for they ran into the Thames, about 200 of them, as we might judge, were drowned by themselves and so were guilty of their own deaths; for had they stayed, and yielded up themselves, the King's mercy is so gracious that he had spared them all. We took there 6 or 8 colours, also their two pieces of ordnance, and all this with very small losse. God be praised, for believe me, I cannot understand that we lost 16 men.[153]

The Butts, just to the north of the High Street, originally the market place, although now lined with late seventeenth and eighteenth century buildings. It was here that the Parliamentary forces stationed their cavalry. It was also here that six Protestants were burned in 1558. (*Author*)

A contemporary, third-hand account suggests 140 Parliamentary soldiers were killed in total, which appears credible. Others would have died of wounds following the battle. Smallwood claims 400 Parliamentary prisoners were said to have been taken, but 140 were released shortly after the action; the remainder apparently enlisted with the royalists. The King, in a subsequent letter to Parliament, claimed 10 Royalist dead. One unsubstantiated account suggests the Royalist dead were removed to Hounslow Heath.[154]

A number of the wounded who were able to be moved were taken to the Savoy, which was by then a hospital off the Strand fronting onto the Thames, 'Where they were looked after by the Master and Wardens of the Surgeons' Company. Those too ill to be moved were cared for in Brentford. A sum of 20*s* was paid to the church of St Lawrence for the treatment of the wounded.'[155]

The Battle of Turnham Green: 13 November 1642

The Royalist army was commanded by Patrick Ruthven, Earl of Forth, but with King Charles I present. As with the battle the day before, the Parliamentarian army was commanded by Robert Devereux, third Earl of Essex. Sergeant Major General Philip Skippon was in command of the London militia. The Battlefield

Trust estimates that there were probably around 12,000 Royalists and 24,000 Parliamentarians present. This was a battle of bluff and counter-bluff that never got under-way, but in the sniping and associated skirmishes, around 50 persons in total from both sides were killed.

Background

Following the Royalist capture of Brentford on 12 November, a detachment of Royalist forces had halted on Turnham Green on the same night. As Marsh says, 'The surprise attack on the Parliamentarian regiments and the sack of the town, when peace negotiations were being discussed, came as a shock ... It had the effect of hardening opinion against a settlement and rallied the citizens in favour of a stand against the king.'[156] The royalist delay in marching on London allowed the Parliamentary army and London militia to form-up on Turnham Green and Chiswick common field the next day. The battle (although it was more of a stand-off than a battle) began at around 8 a.m. and lasted until dark.

When the Earl of Essex, commander of the Parliamentary army, learnt of the Royalist attack and capture of Brentford, he immediately gathered together his forces, called out the Trained Bands of London apprentices (an early form of the Territorial Army) and marched throughout the night of 12 November. By

Approximately 200 fleeing Parliamentary soldiers perished here on the Thames, which runs around 300 yards south of the High Street. The area to the right is an island. The island can be seen quite clearly on the Moses Glover Map of 1634, and the Rocque Map of 1745. (*Author*)

8 a.m., a gigantic force of about 24,000 Parliamentarians was at Turnham Green facing the Royalist soldiers who had arrived from Brentford. There were some skirmishes, but the Royalists were so outnumbered that they wisely decided to retreat back to Kingston in the evening. King Charles' advance on London was foiled and he never again came so close to taking the capital.[157]

In numerical terms, this was close to being the largest ever military confrontation in the British Isles [...] On the east side of the battlefield, the Parliamentarian front probably ran from enclosures fringing the north side of the green to the garden walls of Chiswick House. Musketeers and dragoons placed in the gardens would have secured their left flank. Beyond the house was an expanse of meadows that was unsuitable for troop movements, especially so late in the year, and a party of troops attempting to cross them would have been countered relatively easily before it could reach Chiswick village [...] Essex placed his artillery, protected by earthworks, to cover the roads running across the battlefield [...] The royalist front probably ran from Acton Green across the modern Turnham Green and east of the line of Sutton Court Road. The gardens of Sutton Court on the south side of the Bollo Brook – at the junction of the modern Fauconberg Road and Sutton Court Road – gave cover for troops protecting their right flank [...] The Parliamentarian front extended for roughly 1,200 yards, but the Royalists' line was rather shorter.[158]

The diary of Bulstrode Whitelocke tells us:[159]

Beyond Hammersmith in a lane were placed the great Guns ready to be drawn up as there should be occasion, and a little beyond were the Carriages, in a Field close to the Highway, placed with great Guards about them for their defence. The whole army was drawn up in Battalia in a Common called Turnham-Green, about a mile from Brentford, Essex, had there a strong party of horse, stout Men, well horsed and armed [...] The whole Army stood many Hours in Battalia, as the King's Army had done, facing one another. Whenever either of them advanced toward the other, or that the Soldiers shouted, then 200 or 300 Horsemen, who came from London to be spectators, would gallop away towards London as fast as they could ride, to the Discouragement of the Parliament's Army; and divers of the Soldiers would steal from their Colours towards their home, the City. It was then consulted whether the Parliament Army should advance, and fall upon the King's forces, which was the opinion of most of the Parliament-men, and Gentlemen, who were Officers; but the Soldiers of Fortune were altogether against it; and while we were consulting the King had drawn off his Carriages, and Ordnance, and when everyone spake his Opinion, the General gave his Orders as he thought best. The City Good-wives, and others, mindful of their Husband and Friends, sent many

Above left: Patrick Ruthven (*c.* 1573-1651), Earl of Forth, and made 1st Earl of Brentford in 1644. He commanded the Royalist army at Turnham Green. Charles I was present at the stand-off.

Above right: Sir Bulstrode Whitelocke (1605-1675), English lawyer, writer, Parliamentarian, and Lord Keeper of the Great Seal of England. On the outbreak of the English Civil War he took the side of Parliament.

Cart-loads of Provisions, and Wines, and good things to Turnham-Green, with which the Soldiers were refreshed, and made merry; and the more, when they understood that the King and all his Army were retreated. Upon this was another Consultation whether we should pursue them, which all advised, but the old Soldiers of Fortune: on whose Judgment the General most relied; and their Reasons were, 'That it was too hazardous to follow the Enemy, and Honour and Safely enough to the Parliament that the King was retreated.' But some of the King's Party did afterwards confess to me and others, that if we had fallen on them at this time, they had not Bullet enough to have maintained Fight for a quarter of an Hour, but that, in probability, we had wholly broken them, and this was the Cause of their Retreat. And God had a farther Controversy yet against us. The King being marched away, the General gave Orders for the Citizens to go home, which they gladly obeyed; to return to their Wives and Families that Night. The King marched back to Colnebrook, from thence to Reading, and so to Oxford, his most convenient Quarter.

An account by The Earl of Pembroke, Lord Saye, Sele B. Fielding, John Pym, and Anthony Nicolls, the Committee of Public Safety to the Committees of the Deputy Lieutenants of Hertfordshire:[160]

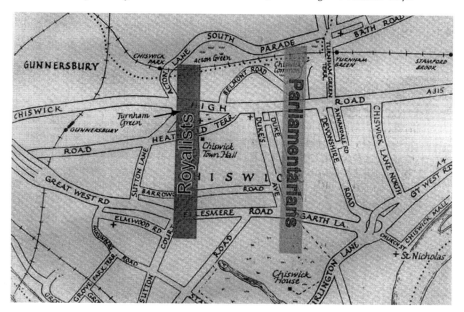

Royalist and Parliamentary positions. The lines begin outside Turnham Green Station, cut across the green, and end in what are now ordinary suburban streets. (*Battlefield Trust*)

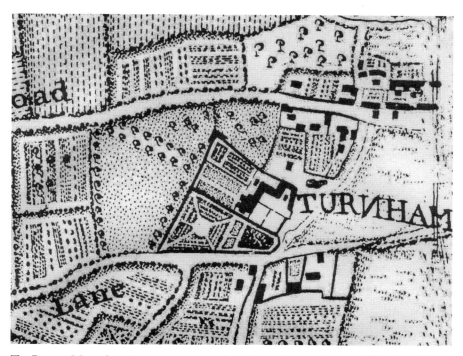

The Rocque Map of 1745, just over 100 years later, shows the rural aspect of Turnham Green. The green retains much of its original shape.

Turnham Green looking east-west. The modern church approximates to where the Royalist lines would have been on a north (right) to south (left) axis. (*Author*)

View from Acton Common end of Battlefield. This was the approximate area of the northern flank of the Royalist army. (*Author*)

Kingston Bridge upstream from Brentford. It was here that the Royalists ransacked the town and held the bridge as they retreated after Turnham Green. This bridge dates from 1828 and replaced the earlier wooden bridge from the time of the Civil Wars. The Thames path here leads down to Brentford. (*Author*)

The same view of Kingston Bridge, 1833. (*New and Complete History of the Counties of Surrey and Sussex*)

15 November 1642

The Lord General's army stood in batalia in Turnham Greene, the other army of the cavaliers and malignants in a close between them and Branford [Brentford] without giving them any charge, though to amuse our men they made many offers as if they would have charged. But about fower of the clock, our men began to charge them with some ordnance, but they closlie withdrew themselves and march away leaving the feild and the towne to our army. It being now growne dark, it was not thought good to follow them, soe they march in a great confusion without opposition to Kingston where most of the horse was quartered, and in some adjacent villages.

The Turnham Green battlefield area is now a mixture of open land and ordinary urban streets. Parts of Turnham Green and Acton Green are now municipal parkland, and they provide a sense of what the original battle ground may have looked like. The battleground extended as far south as Chiswick House in the seventeenth century. Walking the ground, as with Brentford, is now straight forward and rewarding, as the Battlefield Trust have placed a series of 'what happened here' boards. The best starting point for Turnham Green is Turnham Green Underground Station, which is located on Turnham Green Terrace (B491) on the edge of Chiswick Common. It is about 200 m north of the A315, Chiswick High Road. The first board is almost opposite the station.

Above and below: Hounslow Heath. Difficult to locate from modern-day Hounslow, but a Royalist mustering point just before the Battle of Brentford. It is possible that some of the dead were buried here after the battle. (*Author*)

CHAPTER TEN

The Gordon Riots, 1780

The Gordon Riots of June 1780 came out of religious intolerance, and set London alight. The story itself is fascinating; were it not historically based, it would seem in some areas almost improbable. Essentially, it is intertwined with the eccentric Scottish nobleman Lord George Gordon, third and youngest son of Cosmo George Gordon, third Duke of Gordon. He was educated at Eton and joined the Royal Navy in 1763 at the age of twelve. His career in the navy was a failure, but he secured a seat in Parliament in 1773, where he championed unpopular causes, such as American Independence. Gordon, who would end his days as a devout Orthodox Jew, living in the Jewish quarter of Birmingham before perishing in Newgate Gaol in 1779, made himself head of the Protestant associations, whose aim was to secure the repeal of the Catholic Relief Act of 1778. The Catholics, even in the Age of the Enlightenment, were still seen as a threat to the monarchy, being loyal to both Rome and the monarch, a dual loyalty that many English Protestants regarded with suspicion. The riots commenced with a political motive and ended as a free-for-all attempt by the mob to right perceived social grievances and enrich itself by plunder.

On 2 June 1780, Gordon headed a crowd of around 50,000 people that marched in procession from St George's Fields to the Houses of Parliament in order to present a huge petition against (partial) Catholic emancipation. What happened next would lead to parts of London being set alight, the army being called out, and the killing and wounding of around 450 persons. A large number of both judicial and ordinary accounts survive of the terror that came to the streets of London in June 1780. The memories of the riots carried on well into the next century. Dickens set his novel *Barnaby Rudge* in the riots.

The *Complete Newgate Calendar* succinctly and briefly describes the course of events:[161]

LORD GEORGE GORDON
An Account of the Riots in London in 1780

THE origin of what are known as the Gordon Riots, in London in 1780, is ascribed to the passing of an Act of Parliament, about two years previously, for 'relieving his Majesty's subjects of the Catholic Religion from certain penalties and disabilities imposed upon them during the reign of William III.' A petition to Parliament was framed for its repeal, and a general meeting of a body of people, forming the Protestant Association, headed by Lord George Gordon, was held on 29 May at the Coachmakers' Hall, Noble Street, Aldersgate Street. At this meeting, the noble lord moved the following resolutions:

Whereas no hall in London can contain 40,000 persons:

Resolved – That this association do meet on Friday next in St George's Fields, at ten o'clock in the morning, to consider the most prudent and respectful manner of attending their petition, which will be presented the same day to the House of Commons.

Resolved – For the sake of good order and regularity, that this association, in coming to the ground, do separate themselves into four divisions, viz., the London division, the Westminster division, the Southwark division, and the Scotch division.

Resolved – That the London division do take place of the ground towards Southwark; the Westminster division second; the Southwark division third; and the Scotch division upon the left, all wearing blue cockades to distinguish themselves from the Papists and those who approve of the late Act in favour of Popery.

Resolved – That the magistrates of London, Westminster, and Southwark are requested to attend, that their presence, may overawe and control any riotous or evil-minded persons who may wish to disturb the legal and peaceable deportment of his Majesty's subjects.

His lordship having intimated that he would not present the petition unless twenty thousand persons attended the meeting, and the resolutions having been published and placarded through the streets, on the day appointed, a vast concourse of people from all parts of the City and its environs assembled in St George's Fields. The main body took their route over London Bridge, marching in order, six or eight in a rank, through the City towards Westminster, accompanied by flags bearing the words 'No Popery'. At Charing Cross, the mob was increased by additional numbers on foot, on horseback, and in various vehicles, so that by the time the different parties met together, all the avenues to both Houses of Parliament were entirely filled with the crowd. The rabble now took possession of all the passages leading to the House of Commons, from the outer doors to the very entrance for the Members, which latter they twice attempted to force open; and a like attempt was made at the House of Lords, but without success in either instance. In the meantime, Lord George Gordon came into the House of Commons with an unembarrassed countenance, and a blue cockade in his hat, but finding it gave offence, he took it out and put it in his pocket – not, however, before Captain Herbert, of the navy, one of the Members, threatened to pull it out; while Colonel Murray, another Member, declared that, if the mob broke into the House, he (looking at Lord George) should instantly be the victim. The petition having been presented, the populace separated into parties and proceeded to demolish the Catholic chapels in Duke Street, Lincoln's Inn Fields, and Warwick Street, Golden Square; and all the furniture, ornaments, and altars of both chapels were committed to the flames. After various other outrages, the prison of Newgate was attacked. They demanded from the keeper, Mr Ackerman, the release of their confined associates. He refused to comply; yet, dreading the consequence, he went to the sheriffs to know their pleasure. On his return, he found his house in flames, and the jail itself was soon in a similar situation. The doors and entrances were broken open with crowbars and sledge-hammers; and it is scarcely to be credited with what rapidity this strong prison was destroyed. The public office in Bow Street and Sir John Fielding's house, adjoining, were soon destroyed, and all their furniture and effects, books, papers, etc., committed to the flames. Justice Coxe's house in Great Queen Street, Lincoln's Inn Fields, was similarly treated; and the two prisons at Clerkenwell set open and the prisoners liberated. The King's Bench Prison, with some houses adjoining, a tavern, and the New Bridewell were also set on fire, and almost entirely consumed.   The mob now appeared to consider themselves as superior to all authority; they declared their resolution to burn all the remaining public prisons, and demolish the Bank, the Temple, Gray's Inn, Lincoln's Inn, the Mansion House, the Royal palaces, and the arsenal at Woolwich. The attempt upon the Bank of England was actually made twice in the course of one day; but both attacks were but feebly conducted and the rioters easily repulsed, several of them falling by the fire of the military, and many others being severely wounded.

To form an adequate idea of the distress of the inhabitants in every part of the City would be impossible. Six-and-thirty fires were to be seen blazing in the metropolis during the night. At length, the continuous arrival of fresh troops from all parts of the country within 50 or 60 miles of the metropolis intimidated the rabble; and soon after the disturbances were quelled. The Royal Exchange, the public buildings, the squares, and the principal streets were all occupied by troops. The shops were closed; while immense volumes of dense smoke were still rising from the ruins of consumed edifices. During the riots, many persons, terrified by the alarming outrages of the mob, fled from London and took refuge at places at a considerable distance from town. The number of persons killed is variously stated. Many persons, strangers to the attempt, were destroyed by the necessarily indiscriminate fire of the soldiers and militia; and although it is impossible to calculate the precise number who lost their lives, from the circumstance of many being carried off by their friends, it is believed to be about 500. Lord George Gordon, the leader and instigator of these riots, was subsequently tried in the Court of King's Bench, but escaped conviction. There was little doubt that he was occasionally subject to aberrations of intellect. His death took place some years afterwards in the King's Bench Prison. He had been indicted for a libel on Marie Antoinette, the unfortunate French Queen, and the Count d'Adhemar, the French Ambassador, and having been convicted, fled from punishment, but was afterwards apprehended in Birmingham, attired in the garb of a Jew, with a long beard, etc., where he had undergone circumcision, and had embraced the religion of the unbelievers. He died professing the same faith. Many of the rioters were apprehended, and having been recognised were convicted and suffered death in most instances opposite to the places, in which the scenes were enacted in which they were proved to have taken a part. Among them were many women and boys, but there was not one individual of respectability or character. They were of the lowest class, whose only object was plunder. Among the rioters, to sum up the account of their infamy and wretchedness, was Jack Ketch [the hangman] himself. This miscreant, whose real name was Edward Ennis, was convicted of pulling down the house of Mr Boggis, of New Turnstile. The keeper of Tothill Fields Bridewell would not suffer Jack Ketch to go among the other prisoners, lest they should tear him to pieces. In order that he might hang up his brother rioters, he was granted a pardon.

The reality of the events described is that what started as a simple act of religious zeal ended up being taken over by a mob, who in the words of Daniel Defoe was comprised of, 'Ten thousand stout fellows that would spend the last drop of their blood against Popery that do not know whether it be a man or a horse.' The Gordon Riots were billed as an anti-Catholic reaction to the Papists Act of 1778, but were in fact an excuse to take to the streets and riot. What Gordon had started in all innocence as a protest against giving rights to Roman Catholics moved well beyond anything to do with religious belief. The religious mob had initially died away, leading to a sense that the riots had come to a none too violent end, but then as if out of nowhere trouble began in Moorgate. The surrounding area of St Giles was grindingly poor and mainly occupied by Irish labourers; these people were vagrants who provided a cheap source of unskilled labour, much to the resentment

Left: Lord George Gordon as head of the Protestant Association. He would later become a devout Orthodox Jew.

Below: The 'burning, plundering and destruction' of Newgate Prison. This engraving was made a year after the riots. Prisoners were released, and taken to blacksmiths to have their chains removed.

of English workers. The Irish workers also happened to be Catholic; the mixture was explosive. The riots that began in Moorfield were threatening, violent, and due to the indecisive response of the Lord Mayor of London, spreading as the militia, bereft of orders, helplessly watched the destruction. The rioters were now the mob, intent on taking revenge against their Catholic work rivals. Throughout this second stage, Lord Gordon stood back. It is clear that the religious mission he had peacefully set out on was out of control and had nothing to do with the repeal of the Act giving rights to Catholics. He would later be charged with high treason and imprisoned, comfortably, in the Tower of London. He was defended by his cousin Thomas, Lord Erskine, and acquitted on the grounds that he had no treasonable intent. Twenty-five of the rioters were subsequently tried and hanged at the scene of their crimes. These are listed below.

Places of Note

Lord Gordon moved that on Friday 2 June at 10 a.m. the 'whole body' of the Protestant Association should meet in St George's Fields, not far from modern day Waterloo Station, in order to accompany him on a march to the House of Commons to deliver a petition. As Hibbert says:[162]

> St George's Fields was a big open space south of the river [...] then bounded on its northern side by an oak-lined street known as Melancholy Walk and on its eastern side by the appropriately called Dirty Lane. By night it was a dangerous place and only the most foolhardy citizens took a short cut across it unarmed. In daylight gangs of streetboys chased each other around the wooden shacks of beggars and the bushes near stagnant ponds...

Lord Ellenborough, when Chief Justice, lived at the corner house of Bloomsbury Square and Orange Street, before he removed to St James' Square; Lord Chief Justice Trevor occupied a house on the west side of the square. Lord Mansfield's house was at the north-east corner.[163]

The battle really began on the evening of the ... at the bottom of Threadneedle Street where the troops were ordered to fire on the rioters who were charging towards the Bank. As a contemporary, Thomas Holcroft reported, 'The streets were swarming with people and uproar, confusion and terror reigned in every part.'[165] Poultry was barricaded just in front of Mansion House. At the first round, approximately twenty people fell, dead or wounded. Some of the dead and wounded were dragged by comrades into the Church of St Mildred and doorways in Scalding Alley. Scalding Alley is now Mildred Court.

One innocent observer standing on the south-west corner of Old Jewry, just yards from Threadneedle Street, observed that when the militia fired:

> One of the balls lodged in the door-post of the house against which I stood, not half a dozen inches from my right shoulder; another passed between my legs, and shattered the brickwork against the calves of my legs [...] I lost no time in making good my retreat down the Old Jewry [...] The balls whistled along by me before I could turn into Frederick's Place, but I providentially escaped.
>
> The rioters too were all untouched; but a poor fellow who had just come out of Schumaker and Hayman's counting-house with a bill his master had sent him for was shot through the heart. He fell, gave a convulsive kick or two, and died. Another, in crossing the Old Jewry from Dove Court with a plate of oysters in his hand, was shot through the wrist.[165]

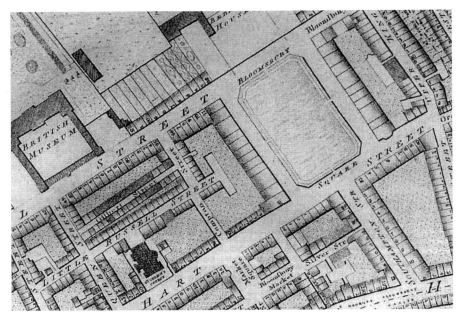

The Horwood 1799 map shows Bloomsbury Square. The house of Lord Chief Justice, Lord Mansfield, situated on the north-east corner of the square, was attacked by the mob. The map is orientated north-south.

Dead Drunk

In Holborn, as evening came on the wind picked up, setting alight houses towards Fleet Market. A contemporary said it 'looked like a volcano'. An unfortunate mistake by the fire engine operators led to them sourcing gin instead of water from Langdale's distillery.

The attraction of unlimited free gin led to a stampede of persons heading for the Langdale Cellar. Soon, the heat led to gin bubbling up into the street where delirious persons knelt on the pavement drinking the raw gin. Hibbert, using an eye-witness account, describes the result:[166]

> Men an women lying prostrate in the streets incapably drunk; some of the women had babies in their arms or struggling near their insensible bodies, screaming in terror or in pain. Several staring, wide-eyed figures lay on their backs in grotesque postures, their faces blue, their swollen tongues still wet with the poisonous liquid [...] below them in the cellars, trapped now by the fire, were the scorched bodies of men and women overcome by the fumes and the smoke, burning to death. And in the warehouse, too drunk to get out when the flames leapt in, other men and women could be heard screaming and

The Obelisk 1-mile south of Blackfriar's Bridge marks the gathering area of Gordon and his petitioners in what was then St George's Fields. Here also were some rioters executed after the troubles had ceased. (*L. Abrahams*)

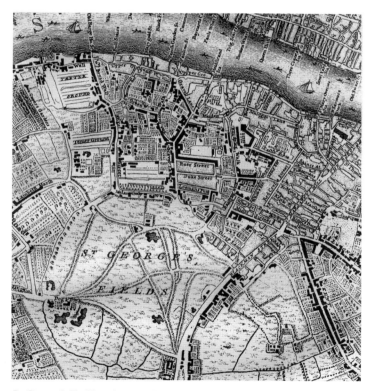

St George's Fields, where it all began, as depicted in a contemporary map of London. Much of the area lies in the vicinity of modern-day Waterloo. An obelisk remains.

Mildred Court, formerly Scalding Alley, where the dead and wounded were dragged by their comrades. (*L. Abrahams*)

Looking towards the Bank and Threadneedle Street. It was here and in front of Mansion House that at the first round of approximately twenty people fell, either dead or wounded. This area was alive with militia and dead bodies. (*L. Abrahams*)

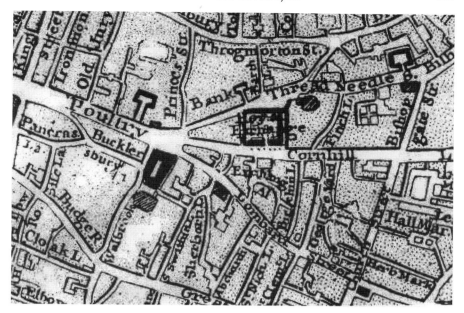

Above: The Rocque Map of London 1746 showing Poultry, Old Jewry, Bank, and Threadneedle Street.

Right: Old Jewry from where an observer commented: 'one of the balls lodged in the door-post of the house against which I stood, not half a dozen inches from my right shoulder.' He then retreated into very close by Frederick's Place. (*L. Abrahams*)

Frederick's Place, off Old Jewry, where Thomas Holcroft escaped the bullets. It still retains an eighteenth century backwater charm. (*L. Abrahams*)

shouting and giggling, scarcely aware of what was happening to them or too drunk to care.

One member of the armed militia reported in his diary that while at the Bank [he] 'fired six or seven times at the rioters at the end of the Bank. Killed two rioters directly opposite to the Great Gate of the Bank; several others in Pig Street and Cheapside.'[167] The rioters attacked the toll collectors' houses at Blackfriars Bridge. The bloodshed was intense and many of the dead and wounded fell into the water where the Fleet Ditch poured into the river. Others fell on to Blackfriars Stairs and were pushed into the river. Hithe Dock and Dowgate Stairs witnessed more death. In Broad Street, the mob attacked the house of a rich Irishman [...] Mrs Hoare, wife of the Quaker Banker, lived opposite and wrote, 'When a large party of the Horse Guards attended by a company of volunteers arrived. They halted exactly opposite our house. Three times the commanding officer exhorted the people to disperse, but they obstinately refused. Then advancing but a few paces, they fired near a hundred pieces and left four unhappy men dead on the spot and fifteen wounded.'[168]

Eyewitness

Ignatius Sancho (1729-1780) was said to have been born a slave on a ship crossing the Atlantic from Africa to the West Indies. He worked in London as a child slave. He persuaded the powerful Montagu family to employ him as their butler, before retiring to run a grocery shop in Westminster. He composed music, appeared on the stage, and entertained many famous figures of literary and artistic London. The first African we know of to vote in a British election, he wrote a large number of letters, which were collected and published in 1782, two years after his death. In his age he was thought of as 'the extraordinary Negro',

Holborn Viaduct. This whole area was ablaze when a distillery went up in flames. The firemen unwittingly used what they thought was water from the distillery to quench the fire, but it was alcohol. The streets were full of drunk persons: the cellars full of dead and dying. (*L. Abrahams*)

and to eighteenth century opponents of the slave trade he became a symbol of the humanity of Africans.

Ignatius Sancho's shop was just a few hundred yards from the Houses of Parliament, and he had a ring-side view of the Riots of June 1780.[169] Sancho wrote several eye-witness accounts of the riots in letters to John Spink. This letter is the longest and the most immediate, clearly written while the disturbances were taking place:

Charles Street, June 6, 1780

DEAR AND MOST RESPECTED SIR,

In the midst of the most cruel and ridiculous confusion, I am now set down to give you a very imperfect sketch of the maddest people that the maddest times were ever plagued with. The public prints have informed you (without doubt) of last Friday's transactions; the insanity of L[or]d G[eorge] G[ordon] and the worse than Negro barbarity of the populace; the burnings and devastations of each night you will also see in the prints: This day, by consent, was set apart for the farther consideration of the wished-for repeal; the people (who had their proper cue from his lordship) assembled by ten o'clock in the

Ignatius Sancho painted at Bath on 29
November 1768 by Thomas Gainsborough
(1727-1788). Gainsborough painted Sancho's
employers, the Duke and Duchess
of Montagu, at the same time. The
acquaintance was a brief one: the portrait
took Gainsborough only 1 hour 40 minutes
to paint.

morning. Lord N[orth], who had been up in council at home till four in the
morning, got to the house before eleven, just a quarter of an hour before the
associators reached Palace-yard; but, I should tell you, in council there was
a deputation from all parties; the S[helburne] party were for prosecuting
L[or]d G[eorge], and leaving him at large; the At[torne]y G[enera]l laughed
at the idea, and declared it was doing just nothing; the M[inistr]y were for his
expulsion, and so dropping him gently into insignificancy; that was thought
wrong, as he would still be industrious in mischief; the R[ockingha]m party,
I should suppose, you will think counselled best, which is, this day to expel
him the house – commit him to the Tower – and then prosecute him at leisure
– by which means he will lose the opportunity of getting a seat in the next
parliament and have decent leisure to repent him of the heavy evils he has
occasioned. There is at this present moment at least a hundred thousand poor,
miserable, ragged rabble, from twelve to sixty years of age, with blue cockades
in their hats, besides half as many women and children, all parading the streets
, the bridge, the park, ready for any and every mischief. Gracious God! What's
the matter now? I was obliged to leave off – the shouts of the mob, the horrid
clashing of swords, and the clutter of a multitude in swiftest motion drew me
to the door, when every one in the street was employed in shutting up shop. It
is now just five o'clock; the ballad singers are exhausting their musical talents
with the downfall of Popery, S[andwic]h, and N[ort]h. Lord S[andwic]h
narrowly escaped with life about an hour since; the mob seized his chariot
going to the house, broke his glasses, and in struggling to get his lordship out,
they somehow have cut his face; the guards flew to his assistance; the light-

horse scowered the road, got his chariot, escorted him from the coffee-house, where he had fled for protection, to his carriage, and guarded him bleeding very fast home. This – this – is liberty! Genuine British liberty! This instant about two thousand liberty boys are swearing and swaggering by with large sticks, thus armed in hopes of meeting with the Irish chairmen and labourers; all the guards are out and all the horse; the poor fellows are just worn out for want of rest, having been on duty ever since Friday. Thank heaven, it rains; may it increase, so as to send these deluded wretches safe to their homes, their families, and wives! About two [o' clock] this afternoon, a large party took it into their heads to visit the King and Queen, and entered the Park for that purpose, but found the guard too numerous to be forced, and after some useless attempts gave it up. It is reported the house will either be prorogued, or parliament dissolved, this evening, as it is in vain to think of attending any business while this anarchy lasts.

...The Sardinian ambassador offered 500 guineas to the rabble, to save a painting of our Saviour from the flames, and 1,000 guineas not to destroy an exceeding fine organ; the gentry told him they would burn him if they could get at him, and destroyed the picture and organ directly. – I am not sorry I was born in Africa. I shall tire you, I fear – and if I cannot get a frank, make you pay dear for bad news. There is about a thousand mad men, armed with clubs, bludgeons, and crows, just now set off for Newgate, to liberate, they say, their honest comrades. – I wish they do not some of them lose their lives of liberty before morning. It is thought by many who discern deeply that there is more at the bottom of this business than merely the repeal of an act, which has as yet produced no bad consequences, and perhaps never might. I am forced to own that I am for universal toleration. Let us convert by our example, and conquer by our meekness and brotherly love!

Eight o'clock. Lord G[eorge] G[ordon] has this moment announced to my lords the mob that the act shall be repealed this evening; upon this, they gave a hundred cheers, took the horses from his hackney coach, and rolled him full jollily away; they are huzzaing now ready to crack their throats.

The Consequences

Inevitably, once order was restored the authorities prepared to take their revenge. The mob had inflicted a serious fright on the established authorities. The Revolution in nearby France caused immense concern. Arrests rapidly followed, including that of Lord Gordon.

Two of the rioters who were eventually pardoned were Glover and Bowsey, described in newspaper records as 'Black' or 'Mulatto'. Both were free men. John Glover was indicted along with several others, and charged with 'riotous and tumultuous assembly; assaulting Newgate and setting loose the prisoners and setting fire to and destroying the prison'. These were the events confirmed by the Ignatius Sancho. Similarly charged as a 'disorderly person' was Benjamin Bowsey, a footman to General Honeywood. The General described his servant as 'a very honest and very foolish fellow [...] that got into idle company' while working in the kitchen of the St Alban's Tavern. Bowsey and Glover were sentenced to death. On 19 July 1780, from the Court of St James', Judge Hillsborough announced a stay of execution for both men. Then on 26 July, Bowsey (who had only been reprieved until 27 July) received a further reprieve. On 30 April 1781, Judge Hillsborough informed the group of rioters, including Bowsey and Glover, that they were to be pardoned on condition that they entered and continued to serve as soldiers in the Corps of Footmen on the coast of Africa.

Lord George Gordon, as mentioned, was tried before the Court of King's Bench, found not guilty of treason, and acquitted. The authorities would take their revenge at a later date.

Places of Execution

The *Newgate Chronicle* gives us the following information:

> Among those tried and convicted were several women and boys; but not one individual of the smallest respectability or good fame; Negroes, Jews, gypsies, and vagabonds of every description; the very refuse of society.
>
> Richard Roberts and William Lawrence, mere lads in appearance, hardly seventeen years of age, were among the principal leaders in these dreadful scenes of destruction, and were the first who were brought to trial. They were convicted of pulling down the house of Sir John Fielding, and hanged in Bow Street.
>
> Thomas Taplin, a captain-rioter, convicted of extorting money from Mr Mahon. That gentleman deposed that a ragged little boy came first up to him, and said, 'God bless your honour, some money for your poor mob!' He bid him begone. 'Then,' replied the imp of mischief, 'I'll call my captain.' Then came up the prisoner Taplin, on horse-back, led by two boys, and attended by forty or fifty followers. Mr Mahon was intimidated, so as to purchase his security with half a crown. Taplin was also hanged in Bow Street, where he had stopped Mr Mahon.
>
> George Kennedy, hanged in Bunhill-row, for pulling down the house of Mr M'Cartney, a baker.
>
> William M'Donald, a cripple, who had lost an arm and had formerly been a soldier, hanged on Tower-hill for destroying the house of J. Lebarty, a publican, in St Catharine's lane, near thereto.
>
> James Henry, for setting fire to the house of Mr Langdon, on Holborn-hill.

George Bawton, a poor drunken cobbler, who meeting Mr Richard Stone, in High Street, Holborn, stopped him, saying, 'Pray remember the Protestant religion.' Mr Stone offered twopence, but the cobler damned him, and swore he would have sixpence, which was compiled with, for this he was hanged! A punishment which at any other time would have borne no proportion to the crime, and an instance of severity which we trust could not at any other time have occurred in England.

William Browne, for extorting money from Mr Daking, in Bishopsgate Street, as for the Protestant cause, and threatening to rip him up if he did not comply.

William Bateman, executed in Coleman Street, for pulling down the house of Mr Charlton.

John Gray, Charles Kent, and Letitia Holland, hanged in Bloomsbury-square, for being a party to setting fire to the mansion of Lord Chief Justice Mansfield.

Mary Roberts and Charlotte Gardener, the latter a negress, hanged on Tower Hill for assisting to demolish the house of J. Lebarty, as before-mentioned.

Enoch Fleming, executed in Oxford Road, for assisting in pulling down the house of Ferdinand Schomberg.

George Staples, for being concerned in the riot in Moorfields, and assisting to pull down the Roman Catholic chapel there, and the house of James Malo.

Samuel Solomon, a Jew hanged in Whitechapel, for joining in the demolishing the house of Christopher Conner.

James Jackson, at the Old Bailey, convicted of setting fire to Newgate.

George Staples and Jonathan Stacy, also hanged in Moorfields, for being concerned in the riot, and burning of houses there.

Joseph Lovell and Robert Lovell, father and son, a pair of gypsies, hanged for aiding in setting fire to the house of Thomas Conolly.

The following, convicted of setting fire to the King's Bench Prison, and houses near thereto, were executed in St. George's Fields, viz. Robert Loveli, Mary Cook, Edward Dorman, Elizabeth Collins, Henry Penny, and John Bridport.

Among the rioters, to sum up the account of their infamy and wretchedness, was Jack Ketch himself. This miscreant, whose real name was Edward Dennis, was convicted of pulling down the house of Mr Boggis of New Turnstile. The keeper of Tothill Fields Bridewell would not suffer Jack Ketch to go among the other prisoners, lest they should tear him to pieces. In order that he might hang up his brother rioters, he was granted a pardon.

Lord Gordon's Demise

An unorthodox person, Lord Gordon ended his life in unusual circumstances. He retired to Birmingham, where he lived quietly in the house of a Jew, wearing a long beard and adopting the Jewish customs. On 28 January 1788, he was brought up for judgment, sentenced to be imprisoned for five years in Newgate for two libels, and then to pay a fine of £500 and find two securities for his good behaviour in £2,500 apiece.

He amused himself with music, especially the bagpipes, had six or eight persons to dinner daily, including the society of Newgate, and occasionally distinguished outsiders, who all dined on terms of strict equality; he gave a ball once a fortnight, and conformed in all respects to the Jewish religion. On the expiration of the five years, he was unable to obtain the securities required and had to stay in Newgate, where he soon caught a fever, and died 1 November 1793.[170]

CHAPTER ELEVEN

The First World War: London's Air War

Probably the most enduring images of the First World War are those of the mass death and destruction that came from the slogging match that was the opposing trench system, combined with the latest in heavy arms used in close combat. Less known is the fact that parts of London were subjected to heavy air raids at this time, particularly during the years 1915 and 1916. The initial weapon of choice was the Zeppelin LZ-38, which was of an immense size, 536 feet in length, which was powered by four 210-hp Maybach engines. It had a maximum speed of 60 mph, and was lifted by highly volatile hydrogen. The LZ-38 was the first Zeppelin to bomb London on 31 May 1915, where it dropped 120 bombs, killing five adults and two children.

No. 16 Alkham Road in Stoke Newington was the victim of London's first ever aerial bomb attack. Although there was no loss of life there, the same airship headed south over Hackney, past Stratford, and killed seven and injured a further thirty-five persons. The raid was totally unexpected. Seven houses were destroyed.

Between 1915 and 1917, 200 people lost their lives in these raids, and much damage was inflicted on the capital. The Zeppelins were able to inflict much damage because they flew at such a height that the air force fighters were often unable to climb high enough to attack them. When the Zeppelins were successfully attacked, the crews, often fifteen to twenty strong, faced horrific deaths. Airmen were not issued with parachutes, so they made the terrible decision of either death by fire or impact with the ground. The airship threat soon disappeared after a number of missions were gunned down. The final attack came on 19 October 1917, in which thirty-three people were killed. As the war progressed, the Zeppelin attacks reduced, only to be replaced by deadly Gotha aircraft attacks.

First London Raid: 1914-1917

Evening, 31 May1915: ten months since Britain declared war on Germany. The first bomb on London was an incendiary [that] fell on 16 Alkham Road Stoke Newington. Albert Lovell, a clerk, and his family escaped without injury. The Zeppelin dropped a number of incendiaries, including one in Hoxton, Cowper Road, which left a three-year-old child dead, burnt under her bed where she had crawled to die. Bombs fell on 187 Balls Pond Road, leaving 'the charred bodies of two [other] lodgers kneeling by their bed as if in prayer. These were Henry Good, a forty-nine-year-old labourer, and his wife Caroline. The same Zeppelin dropped bombs on Bishopsgate goods station, Spitalfields, hitting a whisky distillery and a Synagogue in Commercial Road. The night left forty-one fires, seven dead, and intense anti-German sentiment in East London.

Second London Raid: 17/18 August 1915

This Zeppelin raid dropped bombs on Lloyd Park, Walthamstow, and destroyed the Leyton tram depot. Most of the bombs were dropped over Leytonstone and Wanstead Flats. The raid left ten dead and forty-eight injured, but much worse was yet to come.

Third London Raid: 7/8 September 1915

This time, bombs were dropped on the Isle of Dogs, Deptford, Greenwich, and Woolwich. Bermondsey, Rotherhithe, and New Cross were also hit, leaving eighteen people dead and twenty-eight injured.

Fourth London Raid: 8/9 September 1915

The fourth raid was devastating for Central London, leaving scars that are still visible. The commander of the airship was Heinrich Mathy; his airship approached by way of Golders Green, where he dropped twelve bombs, damaging three houses, before following the Finchley Road at a height of about 8,500 feet. His next bomb, an incendiary, fell on Woburn Square in Bloomsbury. His first explosive bomb dropped in the central gardens of Queen's Square, shattering hundreds of windows. Another, dropped near Theobalds Road killed one person, and one, dropped 'outside the Dolphin Public House on the corner of Lamb's Conduit Passage, kill[ed] three men standing at the entrance and blew out the front of the pub'.

The Dolphin Public House on the corner of Lamb's Conduit Passage. A bomb dropped by a Zeppelin on 9 September 1915 killed three men and blew out the front of the pub. (*Author*)

The clock, which stopped at 10.40 when the bomb struck, is still on the wall. (*Author*)

The plaque in Queen's Square, Bloomsbury reads: 'On the night of 8 September 1915 a Zeppelin bomb fell and exploded on this spot. Although nearly 1,000 people slept in the surrounding buildings no person was injured.' (*L. Abrahams*)

Mathy then dropped three devices on Portpool Lane, near Gray's Inn Road, killing three and injuring twenty-five. Moving on, he struck Leather Lane and Hatton Garden, damaging buildings in Farringdon Road between Cross Street and present-day Greville Street. He then turned towards the city, where he dropped a 660-lb bomb on Bartholomew Close, next to St Bartholomew's Hospital in Smithfield. The bomb left an 8-foot deep crater and obliterated two men who were emerging from a nearby public house.

The Zeppelin then proceeded to drop a series of bombs on Wood Street, Addle Street, Basinghall Street, and Aldermanbury. Attempts to shoot the Zeppelin down were unsuccessful. Mathy's next series of bombs left more death and destruction. He headed for Liverpool Street Station, where 50 yards from the entrance, just outside Broad Street Station, he dropped a bomb that struck a bus, exploding under the conductor's platform. The driver lost a number of fingers, the conductor was killed, and passengers were also killed and suffered shocking injuries.

Other bombs struck nearby Norton Folgate, destroying yet another bus, this time killing the driver and eight passengers. Mathy then headed away, passing over Parliament Hill where he was almost struck by an anti-aircraft gun. He

Bartholomew Close lies alongside St Bartholomew's Hospital in Smithfield. Today it is mostly rebuilt. (*Author*)

then climbed to 11,000 feet, leaving twenty-two Londoners dead and eighty-seven more injured.

The Fifth Zeppelin Raid: 13/14 October 1915

This raid also left scars that are visible nearly a century later. The Zeppelin approached via Potters Bar, High Barnet, and Elstree at around 8,500 feet. An anti-aircraft gun in Green Park fired and missed, although the Zeppelin was well illuminated by searchlights.

The first bomb fell in Exeter Street, just off the Strand, striking the corner of the Lyceum Theatre. One person was killed and two were injured. A second bomb, seconds later, fell on the corner of Exeter and Wellington streets during the play's interval.

Another bomb fell in nearby Catherine Street, near the Strand Theatre. From here, the Zeppelin moved over to Aldwych, where it dropped two bombs, killing three and injuring fifteen. Other incendiaries struck the Royal Courts of Justice. Nearby Carey Street was struck, as was the Lincoln's Inn Chapel, which damaged some of its antique windows. The area of shrapnel damage is still clearly visible all around.

The Zeppelin next headed for Chancery Lane and dropped explosives on

Gray's Inn, Hatton Garden, and Farringdon Road. The Zeppelin was now being fired at by anti-aircraft guns, which forced the commander to drop his last bombs in order to gain height. Over Aldgate, he dropped a bomb that struck the Minories, causing extensive damage here and in nearby Houndsditch and Aldgate High Street. Two more bombs only just missed the Royal Mint, just yards from the Tower of London. Overall, the London raid left 47 dead and 102 injured. This was the last raid in 1915.

The Sixth Zeppelin Raid: 24/25 August 1916

On this raid, Mathy approached via Margate and followed the line of the Thames into London. Bombs landed on Deptford, the railway station at Greenwich, and on Tranquil Vale, Blackheath. Bombs were dropped on Eltham, where the occupant of a house in Well Hall Road was killed. Mathy then released bombs over Plumstead, where he killed a family of three at No. 3 Bostall Hill. Nine people were killed and forty others were injured. Low cloud and poor visibility left the London air defences ineffective. Still, the Zeppelins bombed with impunity. The next raid, the single largest of the war, saw the tide turn.

The Old Bell Pub, on the corner of Wellington and Exeter Street, still remains. It was here that a bomb left seventeen dead and twenty-one terribly injured.

The First Success: Cuffley, Hertfordshire

The raid of 2/3 September was largely unsuccessful due to the weather. London escaped this attack by sixteen Zeppelins. The craft that was brought down on approaching London dropped bombs at a number of points, largely ineffectively. These included London Colney, Little Heath, Potters Bar, Edmonton, and Enfield Highway. The Zeppelin was finally picked up by the Waltham Abbey area searchlights flying at 11,000 feet. It was now that a RFC BE2c aircraft, piloted by 2nd Lieutenant William Leefe Robinson, attacked the Zeppelin in what has been described as one of the most celebrated duels of the war. Zeppelins were well armoured and carried machine guns. In a letter, he describes what happened from his base at Sutton's Farm, and how he shot down a Zeppelin during a patrol.

> I have the honour to make the following report on night patrol made by me on the night of the 2/3 instant. I went up at about 11.08 p.m. on the night of the 2nd with instructions to patrol between Sutton's Farm and Joyce Green.
>
> I climbed to 10,000 feet in 53 minutes. I counted what I thought were ten sets of flares – there were a few clouds below me, but on the whole it was a beautifully clear night. I saw nothing until 1.10 a.m., when two searchlights picked up a Zeppelin S.E. of Woolwich. The clouds had collected in this quarter and the searchlights had some difficulty in keeping on the airship. By this time, I had managed to climb to 12,000 feet and I made in the direction of the Zeppelin –which was being fired on by a few anti-aircraft guns – hoping to cut it off on its way eastward. I very slowly gained on it for about 10 minutes. I judged it to be about 800 feet below me and I sacrificed some speed in order to keep the height. It went behind some clouds, avoiding the searchlight, and I lost sight of it. After 15 minutes of fruitless search I returned to my patrol.
>
> I managed to pick up and distinguish my flares again. At about 1.50 a.m., I noticed a red glow in the north-east of London. Taking it to be an outbreak

Lieutenant Leefe-Robinson brought down the first Zeppelin to be destroyed over British soil. It came down in Cuffley, Hertfordshire, killing all sixteen of its crew.

ERECTED BY READERS OF
"The Daily Express"
TO THE MEMORY OF
CAPTAIN WILLIAM LEEFE ROBINSON, V.C.
WORCS. REGᵗ AND R.F.C.
WHO ON SEPTEMBER 3. 1916
ABOVE THIS SPOT BROUGHT DOWN
SL11. THE FIRST GERMAN AIRSHIP
DESTROYED ON BRITISH SOIL

The base of an obelisk set up by the *Daily Express* on the Ridgeway at Cuffley to remember the destruction of the airship. An eyewitness noted that the airship came down behind the Plough. (*L. Abrahams*)

of fire, I went in that direction. At 2.05 a.m., a Zeppelin was picked up by the searchlights over north-north-east. London (as far as I could judge).

Remembering my last failure, I sacrificed height (I was at about 12,900 feet) for speed and nosed down in the direction of the Zeppelin. I saw shells bursting and night tracers flying around it. When I drew closer I noticed that the anti-aircraft aim was too high or too low; also a good many shells burst about 800 feet behind – a few tracers went right over. I could hear the bursts when about 3,000 feet from the Zeppelin. I flew about 800 feet below it from bow to stem and distributed one drum among it (alternate New Brock and Pomeroy). It seemed to have no effect; I therefore moved to one side and gave them another drum along the side – also without effect. I then got behind it and by this time I was very close – 500 feet or less below, and concentrated one drum on one part (underneath rear). I was then at a height of 11,500 feet when attacking the Zeppelin.

I had hardly finished the drum before I saw the part fired at glow. In a few seconds, the whole rear part was blazing. When the third drum was fired, there were no searchlights on the Zeppelin, and no and-aircraft was firing. I quickly got out of the way of the falling, blazing Zeppelin, and being very excited, fired off a few red Very lights and dropped a parachute flare.

Having little oil or petrol left, I returned to Sutton's Farm, landing at 2.45 a.m. On landing, I found the Zeppelin gunners had shot away the machine-gun wire guard, the rear part of my centre section, and had pierced the main spar several times.

The funeral of the commander, Wilhelm Schramm and his fifteen crew took place at Mutton Lane Cemetery, Potters Bar, on 8 September 1916. A woman was fined for throwing eggs at a coffin.

The SL11 burst into flames and plunged to earth, crashing behind the Plough Inn at Cuffley. Today there is a commemorative obelisk on the Ridgeway which was set up by the *Daily Express* newspaper.

More Raids

The next raid took place on the night of 23/24 September. A series of bombs landed in the suburbs of east London. The Zeppelin L.33 was shot and badly damaged, but managed to land at Little Wigborough. All twenty-two crew were unhurt, and after attempting to escape to the coast, were arrested. On the same night, Mathy in L.31 and Peterson in L32 approached from the south. Streatham was badly struck. The bombs fell between Streatham Common Station and Tierney Road, killing seven and wounding twenty-seven. Brixton was then struck, leaving seven dead and seventeen injured. One bomb dropped in Kennington Park. Mathy then dropped bombs along the Lea Bridge Road, Leyton killing eight and leaving thirty-one injured before heading away. Meanwhile, as Mathy bore away, Werner Peterson, commander of L.32 near Swanley, was gripped in the beam of searchlights: Petersen had dropped his bombs and was heading for home when confronted by Frederick Sowrey of the RFC. The airship exploded. An eyewitness stated:[171] 'Those few moments afforded a wonderful spectacle.

Flames were bursting out from the sides and behind, and as the gasbag continued to fall, there trailed away long tongues of flame, which became more and more fantastic as the falling monster gained impetus.'

The airship crashed at Great Burstead just south of Billericay. Peterson had jumped rather than be burned alive. Many of the crew were burnt beyond recognition.

The Potters Bar Zeppelin

On the night of 1 October 1916, the Zeppelins returned. This was to be Mathy's last journey. Only a few days earlier, prophetically he had guessed that his end was imminent. He was in Germany an iconic hero. He and his nineteen crew perished when the Zeppelin came at what is now the junction of Tempest Avenue and Wulstan Park, just off Potters Bar High Street. By 1917, the Germans were using a new type of S-Class Zeppelin, which could climb to 21,000 feet, out of anti-aircraft range.

Wulstan Tempest, a pilot of 39 Squadron, was flying in relays from nightfall; chance and the midnight roster had it that Tempest was now the man airborne searchlights locked onto as Mathy's L31 and the anti-aircraft batteries opened up. Mathy jettisoned his bombs over Cheshunt, shattering many windows, and began a long westward climb in the hope of getting above the clouds. Tempest was already in pursuit and came up under the Zeppelin's tail, firing tracers along the mid-line of the doomed giant. The L31 erupted in fire and began to fall, while Tempest dodged to stay clear of the airship and returned to his base at Suttons Farm, Hornchurch Airfield.

Oakmere Park, Potters Bar, is where the nose section of the Zeppelin struck a tree. The oak was remembered as the 'Zeppelin Oak', Potters Bar had a population of around 1,000 at that time, and the place where the Zeppelin fell is now the junction of Tempest Avenue and Wulstan Park.

Eyewitness

A reporter at the time noted that when he arrived at the crash site, a crowd of locals had gathered, and armed soldiers were guarding a barn near an old oak tree where the Zeppelin had crashed. The front part of the airship was still smouldering in the branches of the oak tree. The remainder lay in two 'enormous heaps, separated from each other by about a hundred yards'. The reporter approached the guard, explained who he was, and was allowed to enter the barn. In a corner lay a row of bodies, all covered with blankets. He pulled back the blanket covering the first body and the importance of the event hit

Above left: Oberleutnant Petersen jumped from the burning Zeppelin to avoid burning to death.

Above right: Heinrich Mathy, a German hero, lived for some minutes after hitting the ground, having jumped from his burning airship.

him. Lying beneath him was a young, clean-shaven man, heavily clad in a dark uniform with overcoat and thick muffler. The reporter knew immediately who the man was. Before leaving his office that morning he had gathered pictures and information about the Zeppelins and the aircrews who flew them. Young Michael MacDonagh was looking down at the body of Lieutenant Heinrich Mathy, the most renowned of the German airship commanders and the man who held the record for the most bombing raids on Britain. As the giant airship began to lose height and the flames took hold, some of Lieutenant Mathy's crew were seen to jump from the Zeppelin as it fell to the ground. This battle in the sky was the incident the young reporter Michael MacDonagh witnessed from the ground soon after midnight, and the bodies in front of him on were the remains of the dead aircrew of L-31.

What Remains Today

Potters Bar and Cuffley in Hertfordshire are both easily accessible, lying a couple
of miles from the northern section of the M25. The site where the airship crashed
is roughly marked by an obelisk on the side of the Ridgeway. An eyewitness
account describes the airship as coming down behind the Plough Inn. The crash
site at Potters Bar is much easier to locate due to the nose section of the airship
having struck an oak tree that was allowed to remain, even though a housing
estate was developed around the crash site. The 'Zeppelin Oak', as it was known,
continued to grow in the front garden of No. 9 Tempest Avenue. A local history
tells us:

> Following complaints from the neighbour at number 7, who was worried the
> rotting tree would fall and injure his four children, the tree was cut down by
> Mr Bill Crawley. Unfortunately, the date is not know, but it is thought to be
> after 1938. Mr Crawley stated years later that he had terrible difficulty cutting
> the tree down; he remembers the trunk was full of metal. All of which he
> threw away! Numbers 9 and 11 Tempest Avenue no longer exist; the entrance
> to Wulstan Park now occupies the land where these two houses once stood.
> The street sign 'Wulstan Park', to the right of the entrance of the private road,
> is believed to mark the exact spot where the Zeppelin Oak once stood. Today,
> the road names 'Tempest Avenue' and 'Wulstan Park' serve as the only physical
> reminders of the events. The twenty crew mans bodies lay strewn across the
> Oakmere Farm fields; some were burnt beyond recognition, others had no
> burns at all. Eyewitnesses reported crew jumping out of the Zeppelin prior
> to it crashing, explaining the absence of any burn marks. Some bodies were
> wrapped in blankets, presumably an attempt by the crew to prevent burns when
> jumping from the wreckage. One of these bodies was identified as Mathy. He
> was one of the jumpers, his impact causing an imprint of just his head and
> shoulders in the ground. Eyewitnesses said that he had not a scratch on him;
> he was an 'ace' even in death!

Mathy's Death

Mathy jumped rather than stay with the ship and be burned alive. He was found
'embedded in the soft soil, a scarf wrapped around his head in a futile attempt to
break the fall. Or perhaps the scarf served another purpose, since it had been a
present from his wife.'[172] It is more likely that the scarf was wrapped around his
face to protect against the heat of the burning airship.

It is reported that the fallen airman showed signs of life for a few minutes.
His imprint remained in the field. The farmer charged 1s a head to let visitors see

it. An altar-cross in the Church of St Mary the Virgin and All Saints at Potters Bar is made from some of the Zeppelin's spars.

The Zeppelin Aircrew Burials

The bodies of the German aircrew were buried at Mutton lane Cemetery alongside their comrades from the Cuffley crash on 5 October 1916.

Almost half a century later, in September 1962, the bodies were exhumed by the German War Graves Commission, and forty-six years after their dramatic entrance, they made their final journey out of the village. They now lie at the Cannock Chase German War Grave Cemetery in Staffordshire.

Transition from Zeppelin to Bomber

19 October 1917 saw the last Zeppelin to drop bombs on London. Its target had been Sheffield. Realising they had made a 'happy mistake', they dropped their bombs, hitting the Graham White Aviation Company at Hendon Aerodrome

The Junction of Wulstan Park and Tempest Avenue in Potters Bar. The oak that the nose section of the airship crashed onto used to stand where the road sign on the right is now situated. (*L. Abrahams*)

and more of Hendon. Two bombs landed near Cricklewood Station. The massive airship flew too high to be troubled by anti-aircraft guns. A 660-lb bomb landed in Piccadilly Circus, damaging Swan & Edgars department store: flying glass killed seven, and another eighteen survived, but badly disfigured. Camberwell was also struck, resulting in ten deaths, four of which were children, and twenty-four injured. The final bomb landed on Hither Green, killing ten more children and five women. The airship was shot down over France.

As the Zeppelin was deemed more vulnerable and therefore less suitable for raids on London, by June 1917 airplanes were being used. 1917 saw the German use of the twin-engine Gotha bombers and Staaken Giants against London. June had seen the first daytime raid by aircraft on London, carries out by eighteen aircraft. The target was the City, where seventy-two bombs were dropped within a 1-mile radius of Liverpool Street Station. One struck platform 9, destroying three carriages of a train about to depart. A second bomb fell, hitting more carriages, leavijg sixteen killed, and fifteen injured. Two bombs landed on No. 65 Fenchurch Street, killing nineteen and injuring thirteen.

Eight men working on a roof near Liverpool Street Station were killed. In Central Street, a policeman was killed. Next to be struck was east London as the aircraft moved away from the City. Unloading a 50-kg bomb over Poplar, the device struck the Upper North Street School. The bomb crashed through three floors and exploded in a classroom containing sixty-four infants.

The first daylight bombing attack on London by a fixed-wing aircraft took place on 13 June 1917. Fourteen Gothas, led by Squadron Commander Hauptmann Ernst Brandenberg, flew over Essex and began dropping their bombs. It was a clear day and the bombs were dropped just before noon. Numerous bombs fell in rapid succession in various districts in the East End. In the East End alone, 104 people were killed, 154 seriously injured, and 269 slightly injured.

Eighteen students were killed overall. Sixteen of these were aged from four to six years old. The two teachers of the infant class acted like heroines as they got everyone out of the building before helping others who were rescuing bodies from the rubble. Panicked mothers searched for their children, desperately hoping they were not one of those caught in the blast. As quickly as possible, the bodies of the children who were killed were removed to the mortuary, and the injured were cared for by nurses and surgeons and taken to the hospitals.

About a week later, one of the biggest funerals in London was held for the children. Fifteen children were buried in a mass grave at the East London Cemetery, and three children had private graves.

Above: Mutton Lane Cemetery in Potters Bar, where German aircrew were buried in 1916.

Right: A memorial in Poplar Recreation Ground, unveiled in June 1919, bears the names of the eighteen Upper North Street School pupils that were killed on the first daylight air-raid on London.

Bibliography

Anonimalle Chronicle, The (1350)

A Guide to Hertfordshire: With a History of the Various Towns and Villages. By an Old Inhabitant (Hertford: Simson & Co., 1880)

Brooke, R. F. S. A. *Visits to Fields of Battle, in England, of the Fifteenth Century; to which are Added Some Miscellaneous Tracts and Papers Upon Archæological Subjects* [With plans] [electronic resource] (1857)

Bruce, J. *Historie of the Arrivall of Edward IV in England and the Finall Recouerye of his Kingdomes from Henry VI. AD 1471* (London: printed for the Camden Society by J. B. Nichols and Son, 1838)

Burley, P., M. Elliott, et al. *The Battles of St Albans* (Barnsley: Pen & Sword Military, 2007)

Cass, F. C. 'Monken Hadley' [electronic resource] (1880)

Cassius Dio, C. and I. Scott-Kilvert. *The Roman History: The reign of Augustus* (Harmondsworth: Penguin, 1987)

Castle, I. *London 1914–17: The Zeppelin Menace* (Oxford: Osprey, 2008)

Castle, I. and C. Hook. *London 1917–18: The Bomber Blitz* (Oxford: Osprey, 2010)

Chippendale, N. *The Battle of Brentford: The Hounslow Area in the Civil War* (Leigh-on-Sea: Partizan Press, 1991)

Clayton, A. *The Folklore of London: Legends, Ceremonies and Celebrations Past and Present* (London: Historical Publications Ltd, 2008)

Clegg, G. *Brentford Past* (London: Historical Publications Ltd, 2002)

Fabyan, R. and H. S. Ellis. *The New Chronicles of England and France, in Two Parts* (London: F. C. and J. Rivington, 1811)

Fenn, J. S. and A. H. R. Ball. *Selections from the Paston Letters* (London: Harrap, 1949)

Fiorato, V., A. Boylston, et al. *Blood Red Roses: The Archaeology of a Mass Grave from the Battle of Towton AD 1461* (Oxford, Oxbow, 2000)

Froissart, J. and G. C. Macaulay. *The Chronicles of Froissart* (London, Macmillan and Co., 1913)

Galbraith, V. H. *The Anonimalle Chronicle: 1333–1381. From an MS written at St Mary's Abbey, York* (Manchester: Manchester University Press, 1970)

Gough, R. A. *Sepulchral monuments in Great Britain Applied to Illustrate the History of Families, Manners, Habits, and Arts, at the Different Periods from the Norman Conquest to the Seventeenth Century.* With introductory observations [By Richard Gough] (London: printed by J. Nichols, for the author, 1786)

Hibbert, C. *King Mob: The Story of Lord George Gordon and the Riots of 1780* (Stroud: Sutton, 2004)

Home, G. *Old London Bridge* [S.l.] Lane (1931)

Hyde, E. E. and R. E. Lockyer. *History of the Great Rebellion: Edward Hyde Earl of Clarendon* [S.l.] (OUP, 1967)

Jones, D. *Summer of Blood: The Peasants' Revolt of 1381* (London: Harper Press, 2009)

Kaufman, A. L. *The historical Literature of the Jack Cade Rebellion* (Farnham, Ashgate, 2009)

Kent, W. *The Lost Treasures of London, Etc.* [with plates] (London: Phoenix House, 1947) pp. x, 150

Knighton, H. F. and G. H. Martin. *Knighton's Chronicle 1337-1396* (Oxford: Clarendon Press, 1995)

London, N. H. S. G. C. M. G. Nicolas, et al. *A Chronicle of London from 1089 to 1483 Written in the Fifteenth Century, and for the First Time Printed from MSS. in the British Museum.* To which are added numerous contemporary illustrations, consisting of royal letters, poems, etc. [With a facsimile prefixed. Ed. by E. Tyrrell and Sir N. H. Nicolas] (London: Longmans, 1827)

Lyle, H. M. and J. Cade. *The Rebellion of Jack Cade: 1450* (London: George Philip & Son, 1950) pp. 23

McGlynn, S. *By Sword and Fire: Cruelty and Atrocity in Medieval Warfare* (London: Weidenfeld & Nicolson, 2008)

Morris, J. C. *The German Air Raids on Great Britain: 1914-1918* (Stroud: Nonsuch, 2007)

Nichols, J. G. *The Chronicle of Queen Jane, and of Two Years of Queen Mary, and Especially of the Rebellion of Sir Thomas Wyat* (London: printed for The Camden Society, 1850)

Nichols, J. G. *Chronicle of the Grey Friars of London.* Ed. by J. G. Nichols (London, 1852)

Oman, C. *A History of England* (E. Arnold, 1900)

Oman, C. *The Great Revolt of 1381: By Sir Charles Oman* (London: Greenhill, 1989)

Porter, S. *The Battle for London* (Stroud, Amberley)

Prestwich, M. *Armies and Warfare in the Middle Ages: The English Experience* (New Haven: Yale University Press, 1996)

Rayner, J. L. *The Complete Newgate Calendar* (London: Navarre Society Ltd, 1926)

Stow, J. *The English Chronicle*

Tacitus, C. and M. Grant. *The Annals of Imperial Rome* (London: Penguin Books, 1996)

Tacitus, C., H. B. Mattingly, et al. *The Agricola; and the Germania* (London: Penguin, 2003)

Thomas, A. H. and I. D. Thornley. *The Great Chronicle of London* [S.l.] (Privately printed, 1938)

Warkworth, J. and J. O. Halliwell-Phillipps. *A Chronicle of the First Thirteen Years of the Reign of King Edward the Fourth* [Lampeter] (Llanerch, 1990)

Weever, J. and W. t. E. Tooke (1767). [Ancient funeral monuments, etc.], London.

Weir, A. *Lancaster and York: The Wars of the Roses* (London: Jonathan Cape, 1995)

Whitelock, B. and R. Spalding. *The Diary of Bulstrode Whitelocke 1605-1675* (Oxford: published for the British Academy by Oxford University Press, 1989)

Whitelocke, B. t. E. and K. o. E. A. B. I. G. Charles I. *Memorials of the English Affairs: or, an Historical Account of what Passed from the Beginning of the Reign of King Charles the First, to King Charles the Second his Happy Restauration. Containing the publick transactions, civil and military.* Together with the private consultations and secrets of the Cabinet [by Bulstrode Whitelocke] (London: printed for Nathaniel Ponder, 1682)

Endnotes

1. Tacitus, C. and M. Grant. *The Annals of Imperial Rome* (London: Penguin Books, 1996) pp. 328-33
2. Tacitus, p. 330
3. http://www.kalkriese-varusschlacht.de/varusschlacht-archaeologie/
4. http://www.livius.org/te-tg/teutoburg/teutoburg-kalkriese.html
5. Wars of the Roses, at which the Earl of Warwick, known as 'Warwick the Kingmaker', was killed while attempting to flee the battle
6. It was here on 22 August 1485 that King Richard III was killed, and Henry Tudor, first of the Tudor dynasty, became Henry VII
7. http://www.battlefieldstrust.com/page68.asp
8. Available at http://www.bajr.org/documents/bajrbattleguide.pdf
9. William of Poitier's account quoted from S. McGlynn *By Sword and Fire: Cruelty and Atrocity in Medieval Warfare* (London: Weidenfeld & Nicolson, 2008) p. 89
10. 'Deeds of Henry V', Quoted from McGlynn. p. 119
11. Fiorato, Boylston, Knüsel. *Blood Red Roses* p. 182. Prestwich, M. (1996). *Armies and Warfare in the Middle Ages: The English Experience* (New Haven: Yale University Press) p. 304
12. Prestwich, M. p. 304
13. Fairweather, P. URL: http://homepage.ntlworld.com/peter.fairweather/docs/visby.htm
14. http://www.brad.ac.uk/acad/archsci/depart/resgrp/towton/
15. http://www.economist.com/node/17722650?story_id=17722650
16. Gnaeus Julius Agricola (AD 40-93) was responsible for much of the Roman conquest of Britain. Tacitus was his son-in-law
17. Both Colchester and Verulamium also show archaeological witness to the destruction
18. For a well-written argument along the lines of how little we really know about Boudicca, see: http://www.militaryhistoryonline.com/conquestbritain/articles/boudicca.aspx
19. *The Annals of Tacitus* (AD 110-120) Book XIV
20. The North Warwickshire Borough website tells us: 'The village is built on a rocky outcrop overlooking the River Anker, and is on the site of a former Roman settlement called Manduessedum, meaning the place of chariots. Some archaeologists believe that this

was home to the fourteenth Roman legion to which Queen Boadicea (Boudicca) met her fate in AD 60 outside the fort in the Anker Valley. URL: http://www.warwickshire. gov.uk/web/corporate/pages.nsf/Links/67105437689689108025704C004CDAC0

21. 'Highbury, Upper Holloway and King's Cross'. *Old and New London.* Vol. 2 (1878) pp. 273-279. URL: http://www.british-history.ac.uk/report.aspx?compid=45097&str query=boadicea

22. 'Battle Bridge Estate'. *Survey of London. Vol. 24: The Parish of St Pancras. Part 4: King's Cross Neighbourhood* (1952) pp. 102-113. URL: http://www.british-history.ac.uk/report. aspx?compid=65568

23. Clayton, A. *The folklore of London: Legends, Ceremonies and Celebrations Past and Present* (London: Historical Publications Ltd, 2008)

24. http://www.britarch.ac.uk/ba/ba70/news.shtml

25. See Dan Jones' excellent postscript chapter on the sources for the revolt: Jones, D. *Summer of Blood: The Peasants' Revolt of 1381* (London: Harper Press, 2009) pp. 213-217

26. Snow *Summer of Blood.* p. 215

27. Froissart, J. and G. C. Macaulay. *The Chronicles of Froissart* (London, Macmillan and Co., 1913)

28. Jones, D. *Summer of Blood: The Peasants' Revolt of 1381* (London, Harper Press, 2009)

29. Jones, pp. 75-78

30. Froissart

31. Jones, p. 87

32. Jones, p. 89

33. Oman, C. (1906) *The Great Revolt of 1381* (London: Greenhill, 1989)

34. Oman, p.57

35. Jones, p. 95

36. Jones, pp. 95-96

37. Knighton, H. and G. H. Martin. *Knighton's Chronicle 1337-1396* (Oxford, Clarendon Press, 1995) p. 217

38. Knighton, p. 217

39. Jones, p. 98

40. Jones, p. 99

41. Stow, J. *Towers and Castles: A Survey of London.* Reprinted from the text of 1603 (1908), pp. 44-71

42. Jones, pp. 126-127

43. Stow, pp. 258-276

44. St Martin-in-the-Vintry was destroyed by the Great Fire in 1666, but a garden at the site remains. St James Garlickhythe was also destroyed in the Great Fire, but was rebuilt between 1676 and 1686. There are memorials on the north wall of St James Garlickhythe commemorating the medieval London mayors buried there

45. Oman

46. Oman

47. Galbraith, V. H. *The Anonimalle Chronicle: 1333-1381. From an MS written at St Mary's Abbey, York* (Manchester: Manchester University Press, 1970)

48. 'The fourteenth Century: Prior Thomas de Watford'. *The Records of St Bartholomew's Priory [and] St Bartholomew the Great, West Smithfield.* Vol. 1 (1921) pp. 168-177. URL: http://www.british-history.ac.uk/report.aspx?compid=51741&strquery=wat tyler

49. Froissart, J. *The Chronicles of Froissart.* Trans. John Bourchier, Lord Berners. Ed. G. C. Macaulay (New York: Harvard Classics: P. F. Collier & Son Company, 1910)

50. Weir, A. *Lancaster and York: The Wars of the Roses* (London: Jonathan Cape, 1995) p. 29

51. The village was the site of a royal palace of the Plantagenet kings. A priory was founded next to the palace and remains of this can still be seen. The church still contains the tomb of Edmund of Langley, the fifth son of Edward III and the first Duke of York, who died in 1402, and is worth visiting

52. *An English Chronicle.* See: Weir, A. *Lancaster and York: The Wars of the Roses* (London: Jonathan Cape, 1995) p. 145

53. For a concise outline of the rebellion, see: http://warsoftheroses.devhub.com/blog/3191-jack-cades-rebellion-1450/

54. The full list of the demands is available from: http://www.fordham.edu/halsall/source/1450jackcade.html. One of the demands relates to the Duke of Suffolk. It reads: 'Item. His true commons desire that he will remove from him all the false progeny and affinity of the Duke of Suffolk and to take about his noble person his true blood of his royal realm, that is to say, the high and mighty prince the Duke of York, exiled from our sovereign lord's person by the noising of the false traitor, the Duke of Suffolk, and his affinity. Also to take about his person the mighty prince, the Duke of Exeter, the Duke of Buckingham, the Duke of Norfolk, and his true earls and barons of his land, and he shall be the richest king Christian'

55. 'London Privileges: Long Shop in Cheap'. *A Dictionary of London* (1918). URL: http://www.british-history.ac.uk/report.aspx?compid=63211

56. 'Borough High Street'. *Survey of London.* Vol. 22 (1950) pp. 9-30. URL: http://www.british-history.ac.uk/report.aspx?compid=65313&strquery=jack cade

57. 'Borough High Street'. *Survey of London.* Vol. 22 (1950) pp. 9-30. URL: http://www.british-history.ac.uk/report.aspx?compid=65313&strquery=jack cade

58. 'Borough High Street'. *Survey of London.* Vol. 22 (1950) pp. 9-30. URL: http://www.british-history.ac.uk/report.aspx?compid=65313&strquery=jack cade

59. 'Borough High Street'. *Survey of London.* Vol. 22 (1950) pp. 9-30. URL: http://www.british-history.ac.uk/report.aspx?compid=65313&strquery=jack cade

60. 'Southwark: Famous Inns'. *Old and New London*: Vol. 6 (1878) pp. 76-89. URL: http://www.british-history.ac.uk/report.aspx?compid=45267&strquery=jack cade

61. Lyle, H. M. and J. Cade. *The Rebellion of Jack Cade: 1450* (London: George Philip & Son, 1950) p. 9, 23

62. All of the *Chronicle of London* excerpts used in this chapter have been edited by myself in terms of modifying spelling and sentence structure to make them usable by the modern reader. Taken from G. Nicolas, et al. *A Chronicle of London from 1089 to 1483 Written in the Fifteenth Century, and for the First Time Printed from MSS. in the British Museum.* To which are added numerous contemporary illustrations, consisting of royal letters, poems, etc. [With a facsimile prefixed. Ed. E. Tyrrell and Sir N. H. Nicolas] (London: Longmans, 1827)

63. Nicolas, G.

64. Lyle, p. 11

65. Lyle, p. 12

66. Home, G. *Old London Bridge* [S.l.] Lane (1931) p. 126

67. R. and H. S. Ellis. *The New Chronicles of England and France, in Two Parts* (London: F. C. and J. Rivington, 1811) p. 624

68. Home, p. 127

70. Home, pp. 127-128

71. Home, p. 128

72. Home, p. 128

73. Hall's chronicle, containing the history of England, during the reign of Henry IV and the succeeding monarchs to the end of the reign of Henry the VIII, in which are particularly described the manners and customs of those periods. Carefully collated with the editions

of 1548 and 1550. (London: printed for J. Johnson [etc.], 1809)

74. 'Cade's Rebellion to Henry VII'. *A New History of London: Including Westminster and Southwark* (1773) pp. 94-106. URL: http://www.british-history.ac.uk/report.aspx?comp id=46723&strquery=jack cade

75. Home, p. 131

76. 'Cade's Rebellion to Henry VII'. *A New History of London: Including Westminster and Southwark* (1773) pp. 94-106. URL: http://www.british-history.ac.uk/report.aspx?compi d=46723&strquery=jack cade

77. For details of the individual battles including sources, and walking the battlefields, see: http://www.battlefieldstrust.com

78. Burley, P., M. Elliott, et al. *The Battles of St Albans* (Barnsley: Pen & Sword Military, 2007) p. 22

79. 'Milan: 1455'. *Calendar of State Papers and Manuscripts in the Archives and Collections of Milan:1385-1618* (1912) pp. 16-17. URL: http://www.british-history.ac.uk/report. aspx?compid=92243

80. Desmond, S. *The Wars of the Roses: The Bloody Rivalry for the Throne of England* (London: Constable & Robinson, 2007) p. 51

81. Burley, p. 121

82. Burley, p. 27

83. A Guide to Hertfordshire; with a history of the various towns and villages, by an old inhabitant (Hertford: Simson & Co., 1880) p. 296

84. Burley, p. 36

85. Seward, p. 54

86. Burley, P., M. Elliott, et al. *The Battles of St Albans* (Barnsley: Pen & Sword Military, 2007) p. ix

87. Seymour, W. *Battles in Britain: 1066-1746* (Book Club Associates, 1979) p. 115

88. Gregory quoted from Seward p. 53

89. 'Thys ys the fyrste of hys rayne of Kynge Edwarde the iiijthe', from 'Gregory's Chronicle: 1461-1469'. *The Historical Collections of a Citizen of London in the Fifteenth Century* (1876) pp. 210-239. URL: http://www.british-history.ac.uk/report.aspx?compid=45560

90. Burley, p. 57

91. See: 'The Battlefield Trust' *St Albans Battlefield Trail* booklet

92. Battlefield Trust

93. Burley, p. 74

94. Burley, p. 74

95. http://www.richardiii.net/ww%20bo%20to%20co.htm

96. Burley, p. 103

97. *Entwistle Family History* (Accrington Gazette, 1924)

98. Weever, pp. 341-342

99. *Entwistle Family History,* referring to 'Whittacker's History of Whalley'. p. 30

100. Weever, p. 343

101. Burley, p. 142

102. Burley, Peter. Burley told the author that what may have happened was that the bodies were stacked, standing up, in the nearby Tonman Ditch, before being transferred to the churchyard for burial, thus giving rise to the story. p. 142

103. Gough, R. A. *Sepulchral monuments in Great Britain applied to illustrate the history of families, manners, habits, and arts, at the different periods from the Norman Conquest to the seventeenth century.* Vol. 2. part ii. With introductory observations [by Richard Gough] (London: J. Nichols, for the author, 1786) p. 177

104. Brooke, R. F. S. A. *Visits to Fields of Battle, in England, of the Fifteenth Century; to which are Added Some Miscellaneous Tracts and Papers Upon Archeological Subjects* (1857) p. 211

105. Brooke, p. 212

106. Bernard, P. and B. G. Green, *Chroniclers of the Battle of Barnet* (Hendon & District Archaeological Society, 1971). The second and more recent book is D. Clark. *Barnet-1471: Death of a Kingmaker* (Pen & Sword Books, 2007) pp. 13-18

107. Warren, B. *Reappraisal of the Battle of Barnet 1471* (Potters Bar & District Historical Society, 2009) The suggestion of Warwick taking the high ground is in a letter from Brian Warren to the author, 28 November 2010

108. Bernard and Green, p. 5

109. Von Wesel as a source had yet to be discovered when Cass wrote

110. Paston Letters, p. 69

111. See: http://www.englishmonarchs.co.uk/warwick_the_kingmaker.htm

112. Gerhard von Wesel, quoted from: http://www.historytimes.com/fresh-perspectives-in-history/medieval-history/476-barnet-1471-a-battle-of-the-wars-of-the-roses?showall=1

113. Weever, J. and W. T. E. Tooke, *Ancient funeral Monuments, Etc.* (London, 1767)

114. Valuation of the Manor of South Mimms, *c.* 1589. See Brian Warren's article 'The Chapel for the Dead of the Battle of Barnet'. *The Journal of the Potters Bar & District Historical Society.* No. 11 (2002)

115. John Warburton's Map of Middlesex 1749

116. Machyn, H. and J. G. Nichols, *The Diary of Henry Machyn: Citizen and Merchant-Taylor of London AD 1550-1563* (London: printed for The Camden Society by J. B. Nichols and Son)

117. *Holinshed's Chronicles.* Vol. 3 (1586) p. 1097

118. Henry Machyn was a funeral director, lived in London, and kept a diary of many of the turbulent events during that period. Machyn's diary is not easy to read in its original form. I have therefore kept the word order, but updated what he writes to allow easier reading. The diary itself covers the period 1550-1563

119. An early form of cannon

120. No longer standing (demolished 1928), but stood where Hay's Wharf, Tooley Street, now is

121. The Diveling Tower is situated at the north-west corner of the tower

122. The falconet or falcon was a light cannon developed in the late fifteenth century

123. Stow. *Annals.* p. 619

124. 'Spain: February 1554, 6-10'. *Calendar of State Papers: Spain.* Vol. 12: 1554 (1949) pp. 82-93. URL: http://www.british-history.ac.uk/report.aspx?compid=88539

125. From the Spanish Ambassadors report to Philip II

126. Underhyll, E. *The Watch at the Court and in the City, on the Eve of Wyat's Attack.* From: MS.Harl.425.94

127. 'Spain: February 1554, 6-10'. *Calendar of State Papers: Spain.* Vol. 12: 1554 (1949) pp. 82-93. URL: http://www.british-history.ac.uk/report.aspx?compid=88539

128. Holinshed, Vol. 4 (1577) p. 1719. URL: http://www.english.ox.ac.uk/holinshed/texts.php?text1=1577_5331

129. 'Diary: 1554 (Jan-June)'. *The Diary of Henry Machyn: Citizen and Merchant-Taylor of London AD 1550-1563* (1848) pp. 50-66. URL: http://www.british-history.ac.uk/report.aspx?compid=45513

130. 'The Chronicle of the Grey Friars: Mary'. *Chronicle of the Grey Friars of London.* Camden Society Old Series. Vol. 53 (1852) pp. 80-98. URL: http://www.british-history.ac.uk/report.aspx?compid=51590

131. Nichols, J. G. (1850) *The Chronicle of Queen Jane, and of Two Years of Queen Mary, and Especially of the Rebellion of Sir Thomas Wyat* (London: printed for The Camden Society) pp.72-74

t George the Martyr, is situated on Borough High Street in Southwark, at the junction with Long Lane, Marshalsea Road, and Tabard Street

133. This was a place of execution where the bodies were left in gibbets. It was located at the junction of the Old Kent Road with what is now Shornecliff Road, where there was a bridge crossing of 'St Thomas-a-Waterings'

134. Hay Hill is just off Berkeley Street in Mayfair, London, W1

135. Porter, p. 71

136. Porter, p.73

137. Sir Richard Wynn, 2nd Baronet (1588 to 19 July 1649) was an MP and staunch Royalist

138. Porter, p. 74

139. Gwynne, J. *Military Memoirs of the Great Civil War* (1822)

140. Porter, pp. 75-75

141. http://brentfordandchiswicklhs.org.uk/local-history/war/the-battle-of-brentford-1642/

142. *Memoirs and Reflections Upon the Reign and Government of King Charles* (1721). The relevant paragraph is available from: http://www.battlefieldstrust.com/brentfordandturnhamgreen/history/sources/further-reading-and-sources.htm

143. http://brentfordandchiswicklhs.org.uk/local-history/war/the-battle-of-brentford-1642/

144. *Turner's History and Antiquities of Brentford* (1922). In *The English Historical Review*. Vol. 36 (1921). Also available from: http://www.battlefieldstrust.com/brentfordandturnhamgreen/history/sources/further-reading-and-sources.htm

145. Porter, p. 83

146. A messenger boat

147. Porter, pp. 76-83

148. Porter, *The Battle for London*. p. 148

149. The house belongs to London Borough of Hounslow, who purchased the house and its 20-acre park in 1924. It is open to the public, but at the time of writing (2011) it was closed for maintenance

150. Neil Chippendale was the local history librarian at Hounslow Library. He has made a special study of the Civil War in Brentford and Chiswick and wrote *The Battle of Brentford* (1992) URL: http://brentfordandchiswicklhs.org.uk/local-history/war/the-battle-of-brentford-1642/

151. *Brentford Past* (Historical Publications, 2002) p. 57

152. *Brentford Past*, p. 59

153. Turner, *History and Antiquities of Brentford* (1922). Also in *The English Historical Review*. Vol. 36 (1921)

154. Battlefield Trust. URL: http://www.battlefieldstrust.com/resource-centre/civil-war/battlepageview.asp?pageid=812

155. *Brentford Past*, p. 59

156. Porter, p. 86

157. *Brentford Past*, p. 59

158. Porter, p. 93

159. Whitelocke, B (1682). *Memorials of the English Affairs: or, an historical account of what passed from the beginning of the reign of King Charles the First, to King Charles the Second his happy restauration. Containing the publick transactions, civil and military. Together with the private consultations and secrets of the Cabinet* [by Bulstrode Whitelocke] (London: printed for Nathaniel Ponder) p. 66

160. 'Manuscripts of the Duke of Portland at Welbeck'. *Historical Manuscripts Commission 29th Report*. Vol. III. p. 100-101

161. Rayner, J. L. *The Complete Newgate Calendar*. Vol. 4 (London: Navarre Society Limited, 1926) pp. 144-148. The result of the riots was: In 1786 he took up the case of Cagliostro,

who had come to England after the diamond necklace affair. Gor... paragraphs in the Public Advertiser, accusing Marie-Antoinette of p... honest man. He was meanwhile corresponding with the Jews (having had some ... with the Quakers), and became a Jew himself, partly in order to give celebrity to financial scheme. He hoped that the Jews would combine to withhold loans for carrying on wars

162. Hibbert, C. *King Mob: The Story of Lord George Gordon and the Riots of 1780* (Stroud: Sutton, 2004) pp. 43-62

163. 'Bloomsbury Square and Neighbourhood'. *Old and New London.* Vol. 4 (1878) pp. 535-545. URL: http://www.british-history.ac.uk/report.aspx?compid=45212

164. Thomas Holcroft, quoted from *King Mob* by Christopher Hibbert. p. 109

165. Robert Smith quoted from *King Mob* by Christopher Hibbert. pp. 108-109

166. Hibbert, pp. 112-113

167. Hibbert, pp. 113-114

168. Hibbert, p. 116

169. Information courtesy of Dr Brycchan Carey, Cambridgeshire, UK. URL: http://www.brycchancarey.com

170. From an article written by Leslie Stephen (1890)

171. Castle, I. *London 1914-17: The Zeppelin Menace* (Oxford: Osprey, 2008) p. 77

172. A fuller account from the website http://www.pbhistory.co.uk/war/zeppelin90.html. The Zeppelin crossed Cotton Road from the north-east at no more than 30 feet in height and onwards towards the Oakmere Estate. Eye witnesses from Potters Bar told of how 'a gust of wind' had carried the Zeppelin some 30 yards further, on to the open space of Oakmere farm and parks. The main wreckage fell near to an oak tree in the fields of Oakmere Farm. This is marked out by the now private road Wulstan Park. In 1916, this area was part of the Oakmere Estate and Oakmere House, which still stands as an out and out restaurant and bar in the High Street. What was left of the nose section fell on an oak tree, which grew at the junction of what is now Tempest Avenue and Wulstan Park. The oak tree would from this moment on be known as the 'Zeppelin Oak'